# Heroes in Blue Jeans

## Kevin A. Ewing

First Printing, 2012

Printed in the United States of America

A WheelMan Press publication

# TABLE OF CONTENTS

# PREFACE:

THE PURPOSE OF this book is to encourage readers to open their eyes to see the heroes in our midst. The world is experiencing a time when heroes have never been more needed, and almost everyone is looking for them. We expect to find heroes coming to us from afar and wearing capes, the way the comic books describe them. We miss seeing the heroes in our families, among our friends, where we work, in our neighborhoods, and where we do business, because we are not looking where heroes really are. They aren't in Washington DC or London. They aren't in the sky and they aren't wearing capes. They are all around us and they are wearing blue jeans.

*In memory of my good friend Mrs. Linda Beckham: A hero in our midst who showed great courage through her long battle with cancer.*

# IN THE MIDST
# OF HEROES

# HEROES IN BLUE JEANS

TIMES ARE DIFFICULT for people everywhere. Many people have lost jobs and can't find more work while the cost of fuel increases making looking for work that much harder. Other people are losing their homes while the cost of food increases. There are tornadoes, hurricanes earth quakes, fires and droughts occurring in every corner of the world. There has never been a time when heroes are more needed than now.

Heroes can be found everywhere. They are in our stores, in our gyms, in our hospitals and our schools. They are on our farms and our beaches. They are on our streets and in our restaurants. We are in the midst of heroes we just have to look for them. In comic books heroes wear tights, capes and are flying through the air. Sometimes we find ourselves looking up in the sky for heroes but heroes don't fly through the air while wear tights and capes. They wear blue jeans, t-shirts and they are in our neighborhoods. Heroes are everywhere we just have to look for them.

It is easy to miss the acts of heroism that goes on around us because in our busy lives full of disappointments, challenges and successes we do not take the time to look for them. We miss the mother who risks her life and years of embarrassment when she throws a robe over her nightclothes, runs out of her home without closing the door behind her to deliver her child's school project and lunch before the pledge of allegiance and morning announcements have been said. We might be too busy to know that scenes like this one occur over and over five days per week all year long. No one would ever think of these fine parents as heroes except maybe their children but they are just the same.

We might be too busy to see the husband who spends the day with his young family so that his wife can have some time to pamper herself. We would never know that the husband is a hero to his wife and to his children and no one knows about his gift to his family but his wife and children but he is a hero, a hero unnoticed.

We might miss the small child and elderly man helping each other and fail to see how that the small child and elderly man are both heroes to each other. We would not understand that the lady at the bank who treats everyone so kindly, who always has a smile for everyone she meets has just lost her husband and is grieving even as she treats her customers so kindly.

Our lives are so busy that we don't pay attention to the spouses of firefighters and police officers who by taking care of their homes while their spouse are daily putting their lives on the line to keep others safe. We miss the tears falling as they fear that their best friends may not come home at the end of their shift. We miss how in spite of their fears that they support their loved ones in their careers.

We too often miss the men and women wearing good pants on their way to important meetings who stop to help an elderly lady or man on a busy road change a flat tire and never get an award for heroism but to the ones they help they are heroes just the same.

It's easy to see the bad in the world but when we actively look for heroes the world won't seem so bad. Heroes are everywhere we just have to look for them.

# ACCIDENT/CRIME

# FORCED TO BE HEROES

AMY AND ALISON are sisters. Amy was born 22 months earlier than Alison. For the first four years of Amy's life, and for the first two years of Alison's life, no two girls could have been happier. Their wonderful parents were so proud of them, and they had so much fun together doing so many things. The girls had tea parties with their dolls and Daddy. They played dress up with their Mommy and loved to be silly, just to hear their Mommy and Daddy laugh. They took walks in the neighborhood and every one they met would comment on what a beautiful family they were. Everything was wonderful, until the day Daddy was driving home from work when another car ran a red light, and Daddy went to heaven.

At first, the girls had a hard time understanding that Daddy was never coming home again, but after a while, the routine of life took over and they got used to his absence. About 8 months after their daddy died, the girls' Mommy introduced a new man to them. Their Mommy told them that she had fallen in love with this man and that he was going to be their new Daddy. He asked them to call him Daddy, and they did. At first, their new Daddy was very kind to Amy and Alison, but it wasn't long before he became more affectionate than Daddies are supposed to be to both girls, but especially to Amy. A few months after their new daddy became overly affectionate to the girls, he demanded that they return the affection by hugging and kissing him whenever he came near them. At first, he insisted that Amy be more affectionate to him than Alison, but after a while, he had Alison be just as affectionate to him as Amy was.

About two months after Amy's mother and step dad were married; he began to talk about her mother about finding a job where she could work at night. He told her that this way, she could be home in the mornings, after school, and for most school functions while bringing in some needed cash. He even told her that any money she would make could go into her own personal bank account, as he trusted her to spend her money wisely. She wondered why he was pushing her to get a job so hard since he made a very good living, more than enough to pay the bills. A month later, Amy's step dad came home with a bit of good news at least that was what he called it. He told the family that he found a great job for Amy's mother; it was an office job using some of her skills as a secretary and as a filing clerk. It paid well and offered good benefits. She pointed out that all of the benefits from his job covered her and the girls, but he told her it would be good to be double covered, in case anything happened to him. He said, "You start tomorrow night. You work from six PM until six AM. Isn't that wonderful?" She wasn't so sure that it was. She really didn't want to work outside the home just now, but because her husband was so excited, she went to the job. It turned out be a dream job, one she quickly loved and made a lot better. She was respected and enjoyed everyone she worked with, but still she wondered why it was so important to her husband that she works.

One day, a little while after Amy's mother had gone to work, her step dad was home, and so was she. Her step dad asked her to come in to his bedroom as he wanted to show her something. When she entered his room he locked the door, and this was the beginning of seven long years of horrible sexual abuse. He stole her innocence, her youth, her ability to trust, and so much more. He replaced these with fear, anger, guilt, and hatred. As each day of abuse piled on to the last one, the one emotion that became her focus was hate. The hatred she felt for her step father grew each day, even as he told her that he did what he was doing to her because she was a bad girl. He told her that if her mother knew what she was making him do, it would tear her apart. She believed what he had told her was true, so that guilt and self loathing joined the feelings of hatred that she felt for him. She couldn't tell anyone what her step father was doing to her, especially not her mother. At first, her step father terrified her, but the more she hated him, the less she was afraid of him. Still, because of her guilt and self-loathing, she endured in silence all of the horrible things he was doing to her, until the day she saw her step father take Alison in to his room and lock the door. Amy knew exactly what he was going to do to Alison. She fought to keep in control of her emotions, until her step father went down the little restaurant where he liked to eat breakfast with his buddies, and her mother came home from work.

As soon as her mother entered the door, she ran hysterically to her and told her everything her step father had been doing to her for seven years. She finished telling her mother about her real life nightmare with, "I saw daddy taking Alison into his room and lock the door. He must be doing horrible things to her too, I just never noticed before. I am so sorry Mommy. I am so sorry. I never thought he would hurt her too." Her mother hugged Amy tightly said, "Honey, that's okay, but where is Alison?" Amy told her mother that Alison was in her room with her door closed. Amy and her mother ran to Alison's room, and Amy's mother called out, "Alison we need to talk, can we come in?" Amy's mother shared with Alison what Amy had told her, and asked if her step father had done similar things to her. Alison burst in to tears, and for several minutes just cried. Amy's mother allowed her to cry, but needing to know if Alison had been harmed by her husband, she said, "Alison, if your step father did harm you, I need to know now. So you need to talk to me." Alison told her mother that her step father had been doing most of the same things to her, along with other terrible things for five years; two years less than he had been abusing Amy. She told her mother that his abuse got worse each time he locked the door.

When Alison finished talking, her mother was in shock and didn't want to believe what her daughters had just told her, but just by looking at her girls, she knew that they were telling the truth. Both girls looked at her through tortured eyes, and she was silent as the magnitude of the horrors her daughters had just shared with her hit her. Their eyes stared back with a look of fear at their mother. For a brief moment, she felt herself grow violently ill, but just as quickly she had an overwhelming feeling that she and her girls had to leave the house as quickly as possible. She told Amy and Alison, "We need to gather as many of our clothes, personal belongings, and keepsakes as can fit into my car as quickly as we can. Your step father will be back here in forty-five minutes, and by the time he comes to the house, we need to be miles away. We'll go to your grandparents' home for a little while. We'll talk more later, now move quickly girls, move."

All three women ran to their closets, dressers, treasure boxes, photo albums, and other places where they kept their keepsakes. They packed up only that which had real value and put each item in boxes, bags, suitcases, and loosely put items in the car. The young women refused to pack anything their step father liked them to wear, or any memento of theirs that he had expressed to them that he liked. The girls were finally going to get away from that man, and they wanted no part of him to go with them. In sixteen minutes, all three had as much as they needed or wanted to take with them. As soon as they got into the car and put their seatbelts on, their mother backed her car out of the driveway, put it in drive, and pushed the gas pedal to the floor, driving faster than she ever had before.

On the drive to their grandparents'/parents' home, each woman was lost in her own thoughts and emotions. Amy felt relief that she was finally leaving that evil horrible man behind, but she was terrified that he would find her and Alison, and bring them back to him. She felt guilt that she, in some way, must have made him abuse her. It must be so, since he always told her if she was a better girl he wouldn't have been forced to do the things he did to her. She felt guilt that she had been so lost in her own nightmare; she hadn't noticed her sister being abused like he was doing to her any sooner than today. As she thought back over the last five years, there were so many times when she should have known her sister was being abused, but she was just too focused on her own misery. She felt so terrible about missing so many chances to help her sister. She hated herself for letting her sister go through what she went through. Amy felt guilt over what her revelation must be doing to her mother. She felt thankful that her mother believed her, because she didn't think most people would. When he wasn't abusing her or her sister, he was a very nice man. She felt grateful for how her mother took charge of getting them to safety.

Alison was lost in her own thoughts and emotions. Like her sister, she felt relieved that she was leaving that evil nasty man behind, but also terrified that he would find them and bring them back to him. Only difference between their thoughts, Alison felt that if he brought them back, it would be much worse for them then it was before. Alison looked at her mother from the back seat of the car and was overcome by guilt, knowing that her mother's marriage was over. She felt like she let her mother down by being the kind of girl who made her step father abuse her. She knew it had to be true since her step father told her it was, over and over, for five years. Alison felt guilty for not telling her mother the first time her step father took Amy into his room and lock the door. She almost did, but not because she thought her step dad was doing anything bad to Amy, but because she was jealous of the extra attention her step dad was giving to Amy. She also felt guilty because of the first time her step father took her in to his room and locked the door, he told Alison that he knew how jealous she was of Amy and that he was going to do things to her to punish her for being so jealous. She was getting ready to tell her mother the next day when her step father praised her for being so good, and told her that he had never known Amy to be as good as she was. He would remind her of this after each time he abused her. She hated herself, so much she wanted to die.

As Amy's mother drove towards her parents' home, she grew angrier and angrier at the man she thought she knew all these years; the man she loved until today, when she heard of the horrible things he did to her girls. She was angry at herself for liking her job so much that she ignored her own intuition, telling her that something was very wrong in her family. Feelings of intense guilt wrapped itself around her feelings of anger. How could she have ignored her feelings that something was seriously wrong with her daughters for so long? Why didn't she question it when her girls' personalities changed so much? They went from being bouncy, bubbly, outgoing little girls to quiet, angry, withdrawn teenagers. How come she didn't see these changes as cries for help? She remembered how she shrugged off her concerns by thinking that before they became teenagers; they were approaching womanhood a little sooner than other girls. When they were teenagers, she shrugged off her concerns by the fact that they were teenagers. For someone who took great pride in listening to her intuition, how could she ignore her intuition for so long when it came to her own daughters? What kind of a mother does not sense when her children are hurting? It hurt her to think that she had been focusing more on her job than on her children all these years. As she drove along, the tires on her car seemed to be calling out "bad mother, bad mother, bad mother" over and over.

Half way to her parents' house, the sky opened up and rain came down with a vengeance. As hard as the rain was falling, it was impossible for her to tell the difference between the rain and her tears. Amy and Alison stared straight ahead; they were hurting too badly to cry.

The three women finally arrived at Amy's grandparents' home, and they stood close together as Amy's mother rang the doorbell. When the door opened, both grandparents stood facing them. Amy's grandmother said, "I had a feeling something has happened to you. I tried to call you for the last hour, but couldn't reach you. I was so worried." Amy's mother fighting tears said, "Daddy, we need a place to stay for a while. Will you let us stay here?" Her father without questioning said, "As long as you need to, let's get you settled in and then we'll talk."

Amy's grandmother helped them unpack.

When they were unpacked they gathered together in the living room. Amy's mother told her parents what her girls told her. She told them that her marriage was over, that she needed a divorce attorney, and was about to quit her job. Her father told her that the easy part of all this was to get her work and the girls in school. Her father said, "I know of a company five miles from the house that needs someone to do about what you did at your old job. In fact, you went to school with him. He was asking me if I could convince you to move back so you could go to work for him. He needs someone with experience. Call him, I have his telephone number. Getting you girls enrolled at school won't take much. Your new school will send for your transcripts. The hard part is to get you all healthy."

Amy's grandmother said, "You girls have been through years of horror that no one should ever have to go through. It would be a good idea to find someone to talk to." She paused and gave a long look at her daughter and said, "After what you just found out, I think it would be a good idea if you talked to someone too. I know a good therapist that you can talk to." Amy's mother and Alison thanked her and told her that they needed to get an appointment as soon as possible. Amy stood to her feet, knocking a chair over, and said, "I don't need to talk to anyone, I don't need a therapist. What I need is to never hear of, from, or see him for as long as I live. Never ever talk to me about him, or what he did to me, ever."

In the days ahead, Amy and Alison were enrolled at a new school and did well, though both were to be quiet and introspective women all of their lives. Amy's mother quit her old job, then confronted her husband face to face. She told him everything the girls said he did, and at first he denied it; until she said that they wouldn't press charges if he agreed to a divorce and enough alimony to take care of the girl's needs. She also insisted that he sell their house and split whatever profit would come from the sale with her and promise that he would never see any of them ever again. She saw her old school friend and asked him for the job he told her father about. He gladly gave it to her; it was even a better job than the one she quit. As long as she worked for him, he always treated her very kindly. They picked up their friendship from high school, and after the girls graduated from high school, they were married with the blessings of Amy's grandparents, Amy, and Alison. It took the three ladies two years to feel secure enough to find a home of their own. They lived there until the girls left home and their mother got married. Amy's mother and Alison began counseling within a few days of arriving at their new home. They were to see their therapist every week at first, then Amy's mother was able to limit her visits to once a month for two years and schedule appointments three or four times per year . It took Alison a little longer, and saw her therapist once a month for four years.

Both young women went to work right out of school. Amy loved animals and went to work for a Veterinarian. Alison liked working with plants and went to work for a nursery, and has ever since. After a few years, Alison met a man at a friend's wedding, fell in love with him, and was married on Valentines' Day. They had two wonderful children who grew up to be great people, and now each have babies of their own. Alison and her husband just celebrated their twenty-third wedding anniversary a few weeks ago. Amy was happy for her sister when she got married, but was happy being single; though she was not to single for long. Amy spent a lot of her free time volunteering at a local animal shelter. She literally bumped into a man as she was trying to introduce a particularly bouncy puppy to a leash. She was red with embarrassment as she tried to apologize, but he refused to accept her apology unless she allowed him to buy her dinner. She did, and eleven months later, they were married. Nine months after they were married, a son was born to her. Now, he is married and has a baby boy of his own.

Sixteen months ago, though no one talked about it, all three women marked twenty–seven years since the night they left the nightmares behind. In all that time, no one ever mentioned the horrible man or anything about him to

Amy. She had bad dreams about him almost every night, but never said anything to anyone.

A year ago, both women opened up a social network account. Ten months ago, Alison had a request from her step father to friend him on the social network site. She became hysterical and immediately called Amy. All the years that Amy had built up walls so that this man could not hurt her, they came tumbling down. For a few days, she slipped into the deepest depression she had ever known. After a few days, she contacted the therapist who had helped her sister and saw him. On her first visit, all she did was cry. She cried away all the feelings of being dirty she felt every time her step father molested her, and she cried away so much of the physical and mental anguish she felt when he was abusing her. With the support of her therapist, she contacted her step father on the social network and told him that in her state, there was no statute of limitation on sexual abuse. She made it known to him that if he ever contacted her or her sister again; she would press charges and would work hard to make sure he spent the rest of his life in prison. Amy finally felt free of the man who molested and abused both her and her sister.

Most heroes become heroes because they see a need and reach out. Still, others are heroes because they are forced to be. Sometimes heroes put their lives on the line, while others are heroes because they survive under terrible conditions. Amy and Alison are heroes because they were forced to be, not because they wanted to be. They were thrown into conditions that would have been too much for most people, but they survived and lived a good life in spite of the evil that was forced upon them. Their mother was also a hero, and like her daughters, she was forced to be. She became a hero when she took actions to save Amy and Alison. She could have chosen not to do anything, as so many in similar situations have, but instead she helped her daughters get away. When she did, she began the flight of a hero; a hero flying without a cape.*

When we walk amongst our neighbors, family, and friends, we are in the midst of heroes. We can see them if we put forth the effort to look for them.

> \* *Even today, there are far too many boys and girls being sexually abused. Most children are abused by someone they know. It is estimated that less than half of sexual assaults are reported to police. On average, a child has to report sexual abuse to seven people before they are believed. Victims face a lifetime battle with depression, anger, addiction, and possibly suicide.*

# BECAUSE OF A CRIME

PENNY WAS NOT an easy baby to be around when she was two months old. She caught every cold, flu, and germ that came near her. She had one ear infection after another and suffered through frequent bouts of colic. She slept fitfully and not for long stretches. She hurt so much, so she cried a lot. In spite of Penny's fussing, her mother Alice adored her. Alice celebrated her fifteenth birthday two days after Penny was born. Two months before Penny was born, Alice moved in with her new boyfriend. He was a drop out and was unemployed. She was determined to get her high school diploma. Her boyfriend thought that was a good idea for her but he was not interested in joining her in her quest, so he agreed to babysit Penny while she was in school.

The boyfriend wasn't really a bad guy when he wasn't high. He worked when he had to and shoplifted when he could get away with it. The boy friend's drug habit and the fact that he was one of the laziest men in Macon County didn't make him the best person to look after Penny, but there was no one else Alice could find who was home during the time that she was in school. Penny's parents' had kicked her out of their home nine weeks before she had Penny. The last few weeks Alice's mother had begun to visit her and Penny. Her father had recently called and had a long telephone visit with her, but they were still not ready to welcome Alice and Penny in to their home.

Monday morning Alice didn't want to go to school, she had a bad feeling about the day but she had a Calculus exam late in the morning to take, so she thought maybe that was it. Deep down she was really worried about Penny, but she didn't know why. Penny was not crying so much the last few days and seemed to be feeling better, but still somehow she was worried. She got dressed herself, then undressed, changed, dressed, and fed Penny, and then made breakfast for her and the boyfriend. Alice looked at the wall clock and it read 7: 15 A.M. She gave the boyfriend a quick kiss on the forehead, told him to watch Penny closely and ran out the door to catch her ride to school.

Penny began the day quietly after her mother left, taking small naps and crying quietly between naps. By ten o'clock, the boyfriend had a poker game going with four other pot heads. At ten thirty, a friend showed up with some high quality pot and wanted to get in to the game. As a gift for letting him get in to the game, he gave each of them a joint to smoke. After that, it was easy for the game to include another player.

By eleven o'clock the game was really going well. The beer, pot, and cards seemed to be a good way to spend a day for the six of them. By eleven o'clock, Penny was really hurting. She had a full diaper, hadn't eaten since seven o'clock, and had yet another ear infection. Penny began to cry hard at first and then to scream. For a short while the six men were so high that they didn't hear her, but after a little while, Penny's screams and cries began to annoy the drug addled men, especially the boyfriend.

At first, the boyfriend just yelled at Penny from his chair to shut up. When, after several yells, she continued to cry, he staggered to his feet without making an attempt to go to the baby he yelled, "Brat, if you don't shut up, I am going to come in there and make you shut up!" He yelled this a few more times at Penny but empowered by beer and pot, he dropped his cards, left the card game, and went to her crib. He stared down at her screaming, "Shut Up" before he picked Penny up and began to shake her as if she was a rag doll. He shook her from side to side and then up and down. Finally, Penny stopped crying. She also stopped moving. Happy with the results, he dropped her back into the crib. He neither knew nor cared that he had injured Penny. All he cared about was getting back to the booze, pot, and cards. If the boyfriend had looked at the clock, the time was 11:32 AM when Penny stopped crying. He was back to playing cards thirty seconds later.

At 11:32 AM, Alice was in the middle of a calculus exam that she was on her way to getting an A on, until she felt a horrible pain in the pit of her stomach and her focus became entirely on Penny. She raced to finish her exam, not even being aware of what answers she wrote. Alice tried to call home after the exam, but the boyfriend was too wasted to answer the telephone. She found a friend who had a car and explained her fears for Penny. Her friend drove her home. Alice raced in to the apartment, and as she did, she was met with the haze of marijuana smoke and the smell of stale beer. She pointed her finger at the boyfriend and asked where Penny was. "Relax babe, she's in her crib, she's quiet now," the boyfriend said. Penny asked, "What do you mean quiet now?" The boyfriend said, "She was making noise a while ago, but I shut her up." The boyfriend grinned at Alice. Alice ran to Penny and in a panic screamed, "She's not moving, she's barely breathing, she's almost dead!" Alice began to scream. The boyfriend said, "Shut up babe, the kid ain't hurtin', all I did was shake her a little." As Alice called 911, the boyfriend and his pot pals ran out of the apartment.

Penny was rushed to the hospital, barely alive, and put in into the Neonatal Intensive Care Unit. Alice spent hours being interrogated for possible child abuse. As soon as Alice could call her parents, she did, and they came to her and opened their home to her. A warrant was issued for the boyfriend on attempted murder charges and doctors worked feverishly to save Penny's life. Amy and her parents never left the hospital until they knew Penny would live. Penny was to survive, but at a cost. The shaking she received took her eyesight and her ability to walk, or even to crawl.

On the day Penny was shaken, she became a victim of Shaken Baby Syndrome or Abusive Head Trauma. Penny was both lucky and unlucky. She was lucky because she didn't die. She could have been among the twenty percent of babies shaken who do die. She wasn't so lucky because though she didn't die she was severely injured. The boy-friend shook her hard enough to keep her from ever walking and he shook poor Penny so badly that she suffered retinal hemorrhaging that caused her to become blind. Penny was lucky because in spite of the shaking she received it did not harm her brain. She was a smarter than average baby who grew to be a gifted learner growing up and an incredibly intelligent woman when she became an adult. She was unlucky because of her size and her challenges made people assume she needed extra help. Penny would always be small and fragile looking but she wasn't fragile at all. Since her first birthday she rarely even got sick. She was lucky because in spite of the shaking or because of it she had a large amount of determination. Although Penny could not see and could not walk in her heart she could fly like an eagle and see like a hawk.

Penny learned to use a wheel chair to get around her house and yard before she was five. The neighbors next door had a little girl Penny's age who she became best friends with by the time she was six. Her friend, Faith, was so excited about school and Penny wanted to go to school too, but her mother decided that it would be easier for Penny to be homeschooled. Her grandparents supported Alice in that, since they had not anticipated Penny's determination to go to school. They were to learn what a child with a single focus can sound like when she asked for something a thousand times per day, or so it seemed to Alice and her parents. They held out as long as they could, three months. Then they made arrangements for her to go to school.

Penny loved school from the first day until graduation, twelve years later, but school wasn't very easy for her, especially at first. Penny's grandfather observed how hard she worked at home, and even volunteered at school to observe how she worked at school. He saw that Penny worked as hard at school as she did at home, but she couldn't see words on pages that need to be read. After observing Penny a few more times, her grandfather wanted to help her be as independent as possible. He did some research on how to help Penny and found out that Braille, a method for people who are blind to read and write, would help her keep up with her peers. This method was developed in 1825. He found that fewer and fewer people who are blind are able to read Braille, and people who can read Braille are more likely to find employment than those who cannot. He made sure that Penny learned how to read and write Braille. *

As soon as Penny could read Braille, school became easier and her grades skyrocketed. When she entered her senior year in High school, she had a 3.6 average and had applied to four major universities to major in pre-pharmacy. Everyone, from school counselors to even her grandfather, tried to discourage her from pursuing a career as a pharmacist, but her determination was stronger than ever. At graduation, she had improved her GPA to 3.8, had accepted three major scholarships, and had been accepted into the University that she had hoped to go to. In spite of everyone who tried to discourage her, two years later she was accepted in the school of pharmacy, and six years later she became a pharmacist at a well known hospital.

Sometimes heroes are who they are because of situations that are out of their control. They accept things as they are and make the best of what they have. They don't moan and complain about how bad things are, and they never feel sorry for themselves. They rise above the bad things. Penny was one such a hero. According to the National Center on Shaken Baby Syndrome, an estimated 1,200 to 1,400 children are injured or killed by shaking every year in the United States. Actual numbers may be much higher, as many likely go undetected. Every year, about one thousand babies begin the process of becoming heroes because of vicious adults.

* *According to the 2007 Annual Report from the American Printing House for the Blind; Currently about eighty-five percent of all children in the United States who are legally blind and attend public school have access to only*

*a few teachers who can even read Braille. Of those teach-
ers who can read Braille, only a few of them are able to
teach students to read and write/emboss Braille. Only
about ten percent of the children in public schools who
are blind can read Braille. The unemployment rate for
people who are blind who do not read Braille is about
seventy percent. The unemployment rate for people who
are blind and can read Braille is about twenty percent.*

# Traumatic Brain Injury

THE PURPOSE OF the story you are about to read is to acquaint you with the challenges that many people who have traumatic brain injuries have to fight daily, most for the rest of their lives. Victims of Traumatic Brain Injury have long and lonely individual windmill fights. They face prejudices from people all around them. Their friends and even their family members misunderstand them. They may experience sympathy shortly after whatever event caused the traumatic brain injury, but the sympathy evaporates over time. It can take long periods of time, if ever, for full recovery and so as time goes by; the victims find themselves fighting their challenges alone. As you read this piece, please keep in mind that no one asks to have an injury of this kind. This piece was written with deep respect and empathy to those who face the huge battles that having traumatic brain injury forces upon them.

Our brain is remarkable, because it does so much for us. Yet science tells us that we only use a small part of it, which makes a brain that is in good condition miraculous. The part of our brain that we use the most allows us to experience the most wondrous and amazing experiences. A well working brain makes it possible for us to experience the joys and awkwardness of movements. We can experience the wonders of perfumes and odors that envelop us and are able to see the beauties and ugliness of our world, without even knowing how it happens. At the same time, we are able to hear the beautiful and ugly sounds all around us. Our brain allows us to feel the smoothest, softest, roughest, and nastiest surfaces. We know what a warm smile or a cold frown means. A well working brain gives us sweet and bittersweet, short and long-term memories. It allows us to know right from wrong and to make choices, good or bad. We are able to feel remorse, regret, anger, pain, joy, love, laughter, and to be individuals. Best of all, a well working brain allows us to keep living.

On the day Brad received his brain injury, he was a healthy, thirty-one year old man. He had two learning disabilities, dyslexia, where letters changed when he read words and dyscalculia, where numbers changed when he saw them on paper. He'd learned to accommodate his learning disabilities and had discovered that he was quite intelligent. One of Brad's talents was his ability to speak; he was a talker. He never hesitated when given the opportunity to speak, never missed a word and never stuttered.

It was a typical winter day in the San Joaquin valley of California, sunny with patches of Tule fog. Brad was a driving instructor and had spent more time with his first student of the day than he meant to, so he was already late to be with his second student. Brad entered the freeway and before long, he ran into some of the worst fog he'd ever seen in his entire life. The fog was thick enough to get lost in seconds after it enveloped the driver. Brad could not see anything. It caused drivers to drive blindly. After about 5 minutes, the fog lifted a little and he saw break lights in the eight lanes ahead of him, and he stopped his car safely.

As far as Brad could see forward, there were wrecks in all eight lanes. Behind him he could see that the fog was less dense, but as far as he could tell, there were no car wrecks. No car moved anywhere on the freeway except emergency vehicles so he sat and waited. After about 15 minutes of waiting, he turned his engine off. After another forty-five minutes, Brad put his thumb on his seat belt release button, getting ready to unbuckle; but as he did, he heard a car traveling at a high rate of speed. He never saw the car, until later after it crashed in to him.

A few short moments after he first heard the car speeding towards him, he heard the car slam on brakes, so he braced for the impact. When the car hit Brad, his seat broke in two places and his head hit the steering wheel at least once. For the seconds of the crash, Brad felt what could only be described as a funny bone like sensation at the base of his skull where his neck and skull met, and the feeling was to last for about an hour. As soon as the dust settled, there were emergency people there to help him. They asked how Brad felt, he told them just fine. He knew that he had passed out at impact briefly, but wasn't willing to tell anyone, because he knew that California law would prevent him from driving for a long time if there was documented proof that he had passed out. Brad also felt dizzy, but again felt afraid to tell anyone. His brain injury was beginning to show.

The man, who hit Brad, totaled his car. Brad's engine and transmission still worked, and was still drivable, more or less. The man that hit him had to get back to Fresno and asked Brad if he would drive him there, about 70 minutes from where they were. Brad agreed, if they could stop at his home to let his wife know what had happened. When they got home, Brad calmly explained the events of the morning to his wife. She had been up most of the night with their baby, so she was not dressed when they arrived home. She quickly dressed and followed the man who hit Brad, and Brad to Fresno. He parked the car in front of the driving school, and explained what had happened. He assured everyone at the school that he was all right and would use his own car the following day.

Almost immediately after the wreck occurred, Brad felt severe pain in his back; but it was not debilitating, so he didn't think too much of it. For the most part, he didn't notice any impairment in his thinking, except that he felt extremely tired and noticed three big bumps on his forehead. Brad's wife wanted to him to see a doctor, but his traumatic brain injury had already affected his thinking. In terror, Brad told his wife that if he went one direction to his doctor's office, he would drive right through the scene of the accident, and he knew that he'd die. Doctors and hospitals in the other direction were not good, and Brad refused to go to them.

Finally, Brad agreed to go see a chiropractor that was a family friend. The chiropractor based his treatment on what Brad told him. Brad's brain injury was already affecting his judgment, so for some reason, he greatly down played what had happened. Not knowing the severity of his injuries or observing Brad, as the chiropractor adjusted his spine, he did more harm than good. Each adjustment caused intense pain from whatever part of Brad's back he was working on, and the pain wrapped around his head for what seemed like hours but must have been a lot less time. Brad went to him for seven treatments, none of which helped. Brad asked his chiropractor about the bumps on his head, and since he didn't remember hitting the steering wheel, Brad could not tell him how they came to be. So, the chiropractor explained that they were just sinus problems. Brad's wife, sensing that he had a concussion, refused to let him sleep, knowing if he had a concussion, he might never wake up. His brain injury began to be obvious, even to him, when he really became angry with her for not letting him sleep. Brad knew she was right, but he didn't care, he just wanted to sleep.

The next morning, the Tule fog had come back, worse than before. Brad was convinced that if he did not drive in it, he would be too afraid to drive in fog the rest of his life. So, he was among the few driving the freeway that morning, even though he was too afraid to drive faster than twenty miles per hour. It took him three hours to drive what should have been an hour drive. When Brad finally arrived at the driving school, his student had canceled his lesson, because the fog was too thick. Brad sadly drove home a little faster, making it home in two hours, even as the fog was lifting.

Brad tried to teach driving just one more day. Even today, he remembers arriving at his student's home, greeting him, and then he remembers his student saying, "That was the best lesson I ever had." Brad thought he was joking, until he looked at the gas gauge in his car. He had arrived at his student's home with a full tank. Now the tank registered a little less than ¾ full. Brad looked at his watch and it was two hours later than it was just seconds earlier. Brad knew at that moment he could no longer teach driving, though he still drove. Brad was to have one more scare before he totally quit driving for a while. When the realization hit Brad that he could no longer work as a driving instructor and he couldn't provide for his stay at home wife and small baby, he wept. He was a man who rarely cried, but he was to cry more as his brain injury got worse.

A few mornings later when Brad woke up, he realized that he could no longer remember the names of his brothers and sisters, aunts, or uncles. He was becoming more and more afraid, angry, and depressed. As a result, he acted out at the only safe person in his life, his wife.

Brad's brain injury became more terrifying to him as the injury became more evident. For the first time in Brad's life, he couldn't say words that he wanted to. More and more, he knew in his mind what he wanted to say, but when he tried to say his thoughts, he couldn't think of the words to say that reflected those same thoughts. Sometimes, after he would say, "uh uh uh uh" for minutes at a time, the words he wanted would come; and when they did, more times than not, Brad would stutter the words. Twenty years later, especially when he is stressed or tired, he still battles this, and still finds himself frustrated, even as it did those long years ago. Along with the words that wouldn't come to him, his face would twitch as he tried so hard to bring the words to his mouth. The twitch he began to do because of his brain injury in 1991, continues even today.

Within a week of the wreck, every time he took a breath, he smelled a strong metallic coppery smell that would not leave him until he fell into a troubled sleep. This was to last ten years and comes back to him, off and on, even today.

After about two weeks of a steady increase in symptoms of Traumatic Brain Injury and ever increasing back pain, Brad's wife did not give him a choice, they went to see a doctor. He was told it was too late for anything the doctor or hospital could do to help his brain injury. To reduce the damage done or to even reduce some of the symptoms of his head injury, Brad needed to be seen by a doctor within twenty-four hours of the injury. After two weeks, Brad could only stand at a ninety-degree angle. The doctor referred Brad to a physical therapist that could and did help him with his back. He was to spend four of seven days, four hours per day, for the next six months at his physical therapist.

Brad's brain injury conflicted with his pride; he down played the extent of his injuries to his family, friends and neighbors. Since his wife had a small baby and was a stay at home mom, it was Brad's responsibility to take care of his family. He could not physically and mentally take care of his family, but no one knew it, except his wife. For many years, friends and neighbors who knew Brad thought he had spent six months being lazy. Some of his very close friends grew to be more distant to him, and for a few the distance never reclaimed the closeness that once was there.

During the time in the days after Brad had his brain injury, a lot of the roads he drove on were country roads, and Brad was unwilling to quit driving until the night that he was driving on a quiet country road and suddenly be-came aware of his wife screaming at him. Brad came two inches away from a head on collision with a truck. They stopped the car seconds later, Brad and his wife switched seats, and for the next six months, Brad did not drive at all.

Brad was out of work for six months. One day they became desperate enough to apply for food stamps. Their baby needed formula, and after months without money coming in, they didn't have any money to buy even one can of formula. Applying for food stamps was an act of a desperate couple, but they humbled themselves and went to the welfare office to ask for help. They waited seven hours for help, having to endure the stares and touches to their baby by some who were mentally ill. When they fi-nally were seen by a social worker, they were told in order to get help; Brad would have to guarantee that he would not be working for six months. Brad said, "I can't say yes to that. As soon as I can, I want to be working again." The social worker then said, "Very well then, no help." For the first and only time during the ordeal, Brad's wife burst into tears and cried, "My baby has no food, we need help, we are desperate. What are we going to do?" She then just sobbed. Brad watched his wife, knowing that he should do more, but wasn't able to. He felt so much guilt and helplessness. The social worker then said, "Here are some telephone numbers for some private agencies. Maybe they can help you a little." It was a private organization that kept them from starving and kept their electricity on.

Brad had and still, to this day, has Traumatic Brain Injury. A brain injury just doesn't disappear; the scars last a lifetime. Some who have Traumatic Brain Injury have a few life challenges, some have a great many, but everyone who has Traumatic Brain Injury face the challenges of life that few can understand or empathize with. If you are not a victim of traumatic brain injury, or know someone that has, it is likely that one day Traumatic Brain Injury will affect you one way or another. If you know someone who is a victim of Traumatic Brain Injury, please reach out to them, be patient with them, support, and love them. Don't leave them and don't try to reason with them, as they may not have healed enough to reason with anyone. Don't stop caring for them, even if it seems as if healing is taking a long time. They may never completely heal, but you're caring and kindness will make a difference in their lives.

A hero has been described as someone who has great strength and courage. A victim of Traumatic Brain Injury who has to deal with the challenges of daily life, make choices every day to battle on, to find ways over, around, and under the effects of Traumatic Brain Injury. We work with, do business with, and relax with these heroes. We are in the midst of heroes; all we have to do is to look for them.

*According to Rosenthal et. al. 1990, (in Brookshire, 1997), about 7 million people in the United States suffer traumatic brain injury (TBI) each year. We are in the midst of about seven million heroes who have traumatic brain injury.*

# LOVE & DEATH

# WHEN LOVE DIED

SHERI IS THIRTY-THREE years old. She has two children. Amy Lynn is four and three quarters years old. She is as cute and as smart a little girl as there could be found anywhere. Amy Lynn has a little brother. His name is Charles Richard Allen III but Sheri calls him Chucky boy. He is two and a half. He is a handsome little man full of curiosity and talks nonstop usually beginning each sentence with the word "Why". Sometimes he listens to the answer sometimes he doesn't.

Up until six months ago Sheri was married to Dr. Charles Richard Allen II. He is a general surgeon like his father Dr. Charles Richard Allen I. He became a surgeon two years ago. Sheri and Dr. Charles Richard Allen II were high school sweet hearts. They were married right out of High school when they were both eighteen. When he began college so did she. For a semester he didn't say anything to her for or against her being in college with him. She majored in biology. He majored in pre-med. Her 1$^{st}$ semester grade point average was a 3.83. His grade point average was 3.75. He was going to be a surgeon like his father. She wasn't sure what she wanted to do after she earned her bachelor's of science degree.

Even with student loans, scholarships and grants there were expenses they both had that they needed extra money for. Sheri found a job waitressing at a restaurant near campus. Very soon after Shari started waitressing she started getting good tips and was making more money than she thought she ever would as a waitress. Her money was able to take care of everything that they needed money for and even gave them enough money to have fun once a week. It wasn't long before her boss noticed how well she took care of the tables she waited. He gave her more and more hours. It was harder and harder for her to keep up with her school work and studies.

The restaurant was doing quite well just being open for dinner. He decided to open for lunch with just Sheri and another waitress working tables. He asked her if she would work the lunch. He was even willing to give her a small raise if she would work lunch. Sheri liked her boss and waitressing. She agreed to work lunch. By waiting tables at lunch Sheri made a great deal more money.

The problem with working lunch for Sheri was that when she waitressed just for dinner she could keep up with her classes barely but she was able to. When she waitressed at lunch time not only was she behind on her work she even missed going to her classes more than just a few times. Sheri had a decision to make. She could either quit waitressing or quit school she just didn't see another way out. She talked to Charles about what she should do. He said, "Look you are making good money as a waitress considering that there is no real talent involved in being a waitress. Since you are going to be the wife of a doctor, your waitressing will really help make things easier for me. Besides you really didn't like college that much any ways." Sheri went down to the registrar's office that afternoon and withdrew from college.

A month after Sheri withdrew from college the restaurant wasn't that busy so her tips were smaller. Hey felt the loss of money. Charles told her to look for a waitressing job at a restaurant that served breakfast. It took Sheri a couple of months but soon she was working at a different restaurant serving breakfast. Their income rose. Charles was very happy with Sheri. Sheri liked her work but had little time for herself. She didn't worry so much about that figuring the time to sacrifice was when she was young. After Charles became a doctor Sheri could take a breather or two and be glad that she had worked so hard when she was young.

While Charles was an undergraduate life was good. They didn't have a lot of money but they were so much in love. Sheri felt so happy. Things began to change when Charles entered medical school. He began to spend more and more time at the hospital. He developed more and more friends who she did not know. On the rare times when Charles would invite her to join his new friends for a drink or a meal she would feel lost. Sheri was always shy but being among all the doctors and nurses she felt lost. Charles made it a point to always bring up the fact that Sheri was a waitress every time she joined him. His new friends were nice, they would briefly ask her a polite question or two but then everyone except Shari would discuss some sort of a medical procedure or something that happened at the hospital and Sheri would sink back in to a feeling of "I don't belong."

A few times others would bring along dates, husbands or wives who were not in the medical profession but they were talented in their own right. Sheri remembers meeting an architect who was a girlfriend of one of the doctors. She remembers a professional baseball player who was a husband of a nurse. She remembers an author who was a girlfriend of a doctor. She remembers an engineer who was a good friend of a surgeon. The only one who Sheri remembers meeting who didn't have a college education was a friend of a doctor who ran her own businesses, a high end hair salon. Sheri didn't feel like she had anything in common with anyone who Charles knew and socialized with.

When Charles became a Resident he spent more and more time at the hospital. Being together was becoming more and more difficult. Sheri continued to waitress. She was offered a job at an upscale restaurant for more money and since the meals were expensive she knew the tips would be bigger. Sheri wanted to talk to Charles about it but he wasn't around. She was still friends with her old boss and still worked for him at lunch and dinner time. She went to him for advice. Her boss was a good man. As much as her old boss hated to lose her he knew that he couldn't do as well for her as the other restaurant could. After talking it over with her old boss Sheri took the new job but kept working for her old boss at lunch. Her boss had become a friend and she didn't have too many of them.

Sheri felt like all she was doing was working, sleeping and not much eating. On top of that when Charles did come home he was either too tired to talk or too focused on the hospital. She knew his residency meant that Charles was getting closer and closer to being Dr. Charles Richard Allen II. All the loneliness and all of the hours that she worked would soon be time and effort well spent.

For a while Charles was so preoccupied with his own thoughts that not only didn't he seem to want to be intimate with Sheri he didn't want to even touch her much. One Thursday Charles called Sheri and told her that he won some money at a poker game and wanted to take her to a romantic getaway he knew about. He asked her to get the time off. She did and took some of her hard earned money to do something that she almost never did. She bought some new clothes that she knew he would like. From the moment he saw her he couldn't keep his hands off of her. The weekend was one of the best weekends of their marriage.

Nine months later Sheri had Amy Lynn. Charles was a bit disappointed that she did not give him a boy but for a four days Charles was attentive to Sheri and Amy Lynn and for a week they looked like an ideal family. After a week Charles was back at the hospital. He came home more often for a few months than he did before Sheri became pregnant and always spent most of his time with Amy Lynn. Sheri's mother lived about ninety minutes away. She helped out with Amy Lynn whenever she could.

For twenty seven months after Amy Lynn was born Sheri rarely saw Charles though she tried countless times to meet with him at the hospital. She had begun to hear rumors of another woman who was seen a lot with Charles at the hospital but Sheri was so busy waitressing and raising Amy Lynn that she didn't have time to do anything other than worry about Dr. Charles. It seemed as though Charles no longer wanted or needed Sheri but then without warning Charles called Sheri up and told her to get time off and take Amy Lynn to her mother's house as this was the only weekend that he would have for them as a couple for a long while. Sheri called in to her bosses and got the time off. She called her mother who gladly took in Amy Lynn. This was another weekend that Sheri felt loved and cherished.

Nine months later, twenty seven months after Amy Lynn was born Charles Richard Allen III or Chucky Boy was born. For a month Dr. Charles came home at least three days per week to play with his new son. Dr. Charles was very proud of his new son and unlike Amy Lynn Dr. Charles had Sheri bring Charles Richard Allen III to the hospital. It was OK that Amy Lynn came too but Dr. Charles was proudest of his son.

Things at the hospital became even busier as Dr. Charles prepared to take his surgical boards. He came home one time to tell Sheri that he passed his surgical boards. Sheri expressed her joy and went to give him a hug. He side stepped her hug and told her that he had to hurry back to the hospital. She asked him what he would do after he completed his residency. He told her that he wasn't sure but for a little while any way he wanted Sheri and the children to continue to live in the apartment. He thought maybe that he would accept a position out of state but he would go there first to see if it would be a good place for all of them before he would consider moving the family there.

As he got nearer to completing his residency he no longer even attempted to come home even for his clothes. Sheri thought that he might have bought new clothes and kept them at the hospital or at a friend's house. He came home fewer and fewer days or even nights. Sheri had heard that Dr. Charles had accepted a position at a teaching hospital two states away but she didn't know for certain only what she heard from a friend of a friend.

Just before graduation, for Dr. Charles Richard Allen II came home and spent a week with Sheri which was the longest time that he had ever spent them. To make him want to be with them more Sheri and her mother went clothes for her and the children. Sheri hadn't bought anything for herself in a very long time. They picked the best days to go shopping finding bargains every where they went. As Sheri looked at herself in a mirror she thought that she still looked good. It had taken her some months but she had lost all of the weight that she had gained during her pregnancies and she still looked good. Her new clothes helped draw attention to her. She felt like that she and her children would not disappoint her husband with how they looked.

Sheri was glad that she had a chance to shop with her children. Shopping with them gave her a chance to see them in a way that working three jobs hadn't allowed her to see before. She was able to see how smart they both were, how fun and how funny they were. She realized that though they were still young children how eager they were to please. She was proud of them. She wished that Dr. Charles would spend more time with them to get to know them as well as she did. She knew that if he took even a third as much time as he did with his patients he would love them just as much as she did. His children were a little afraid of him but Sheri knew that they would stop being afraid of him and love him if he would just spend a little time with them. She hoped he would now that he was a doctor. Sadly he told her that he had to go to his new hospital two states away. She hoped that he would make time in the months ahead but she was afraid that those days might never quite come.

Sheri loved her husband but more and more she wondered if he was still in love with her. It was hard to ignore the rumors and the long nights he spent away from her. Dr. Charles father and his mother were very proud of him. They were so proud of him that they opened their home for a community celebration and family reunion to celebrate Dr. Charles' graduation from medical school and becoming a surgeon like his father. Their celebration lasted three days. Dr. Charles was the life of the party for all of three days. His parents were proud of him and he in turn was proud of his children. Dr. Charles had never been so charming. Sheri's aunts, uncles and family members told her how lucky she was to be married to Dr. Charles. For the three days of celebration she felt that she was very lucky.

Dr. Charles left Sheri and the children two days after he graduated and became a surgeon. He came back three months after he left. He packed up a lot of his things that he thought was important. Sheri asked him when he thought that she should go to the town where his hospital was to look for a new place for them to live. Two months later he came back to visit with a hospital dietician who was just twenty-three. He seemed to touch her a lot. Sheri even saw him holding hands with her a time or two but refused to touch her.

Sheri told Dr. Charles that she and her children were moving in with her mother as they rarely saw him and he rarely helped them financially. He promised to send them more money but thought that living with her mother was a good idea.

Six months ago Sheri and Dr. Charles Richard Allen II were officially divorced. Five months ago Dr. Charles Richard Allen II and the young dietician he met at the hospital he does his surgery at. Sheri was granted full custody of Amy Lynn and Charles Richard Allen III by the judge based upon his full surgery schedule. Three months ago Sheri and her old boss opened a new restaurant forcing her to quit her lunch and dinner waitressing. She loves waiting tables too much to quit her breakfast waitressing job. Already her new restaurant is the talk of the town and is busy every night. She has been too busy to even date. She feels that here will be time for that later. Sheri still likes Dr. Charles and hopes that he will one day have time for his children.

Heroes sacrifice all for the greater good. Sheri did not become a waitress because it was her dream job or quit college because she didn't enjoy college or couldn't keep up with the work. She became a waitress and quit college to help her husband, out of love for him. Her focus for her life was on helping her husband but her efforts weren't enough. Through no fault of her own she was forced to raise two children by herself. She became mother and fa-

ther to her children because her children were so important to her.

All mothers are heroes but single mothers are even
more so. They are expected to do everything two parents
do while not allowing their children to see how discouraged and tired they can be. Heroes face difficult experiences alone. Heroes never expect anything in return and
heroes put their lives on the line for the sake of others. *The
divorce rate for surgeons is thirty-three percent.* According to infoplease.com there are almost ten million single
mothers in the United States. We are in the midst of heroes
and almost ten million of them are single mothers.

# Because Of Love

JONATHAN IS AT the hospital facing something he not only never wanted to face or ever really thought he would have to face. His wife, Mariann, is lying in a hospital bed as she has been for the past forty-four hours. She is a victim of a hit and run driver. She was run over by a speeding car as she crossed the street at the cross walk. The police think that she saw the car at the last moment, because when she was hit, she was almost at the curb. She has very little brain activity that will cease when life support is turned off.

Jonathan and Mariann have a lot in common. They are both only children born to older parents. Both sets of parents have passed away in the last twelve years. Mariann's mother died less than a year ago. Jonathan and Mariann's parents were well loved when they were alive and are deeply missed since they've been gone. Jonathan and Mariann are the same age, forty-three.

They have been married for twenty-two years, and just celebrated their twenty-second anniversary two days ago. Memories of that day fill his grief stricken heart with warm memories in spite of his tears. He remembers how they enjoyed sharing memories of their wonderful life together, with their only child Tara, twenty years of age. They reminisced of how they met in the back of an economics class in college. He had fallen asleep in class with his head on his arms and started to snore loudly. She was annoyed by his snoring and reached over and pushed his arms to the side, causing his head to hit the desk and waking him up. He came to staring at the most beautiful girl he had ever seen. He wasn't sure if he was still dreaming. He looked so confused that she burst out laughing, causing the professor to stop his lecture and glare at her. From that moment on, when they weren't in class, they were together. Tara never got tired of hearing them reminisce. It wasn't so much that she enjoyed their stories, but that she enjoyed watching the way they looked at each other when they told the stories.

They got married a week after they both graduated, at age twenty-one. Both had job offers before they graduated, she as an elementary school music teacher at a school in a town across the state from the college, and he as a chemist, only fifteen miles away from the elementary school. They bought a house in a middle class neighborhood between the two jobs, and two years later, Mariann became pregnant. She had such a difficult pregnancy that her doctor advised her against getting pregnant again. They always said that because they could only have one child, God gave them the best. She was a nearly perfect little girl and is a beautiful young woman.

Jonathan and Tara gazed down on Mariann's almost lifeless body, with the sounds of life support in the background. Jonathan said, "Tara, you know just before we went to bed on our anniversary, your mother and I talked about this." Tara asked, "About Mom getting hit by a car?" "No, about if something should happen to either one of us that we didn't want to be resuscitated, especially if it meant that our quality of life would be destroyed," Jonathan said. He looked down on his wife and gently caressed her hand and arm. Tara said, "Daddy, I support you in this. Mom would not want to be kept alive like she is."

Jonathan said, "How can I? Your mother means everything to me. She and you make life worth living for me. I am at a crossroad here, Tara. If I don't ask the doctors to turn her life support off, the only ones who would know or care are you and I. She will still be with me on the top of the earth. If I do ask the doctors to turn the life support off and change my mind, it will be too late for them to undo my order." Tara asked, "Daddy, isn't love about respecting the one you love? Was there anything you wouldn't do for her if you could when she asked you before her accident?" He said no there wasn't. Tara said, "Then since you love her so dearly, you must respect her last request, as I know she would for you. You are at a crossroad, but this is a crossroad only you must decide which way to go. I will support whatever you decide."

Tara hugged her dad tightly as their tears fell together. Jonathan was glad for her support, but he felt numb and a million miles away from everyone in the world. The only sounds were the sounds of the life support keeping Mariann alive. The doctor approached Jonathan and Tara quietly. Jonathan felt the doctor's presence before he could focus. In a whisper Jonathan said, "Doctor, Mariann had asked that she not be resuscitated if something happened to her. She wouldn't want to live like this. I am asking you to stop her life support."*

Heroes give of themselves, putting their thoughts and wants behind others. The act of keeping a promise, even when it means something or someone will be taken from you, is nothing short of heroic. It comes at a great cost. Every day in hospitals across the country around the world, for a variety of reasons, there are Jonathan's or Tara's faced with the same crossroad that they were. No matter what they decide to do, even if they do not honor a promise made, their lives are changed forever. For those who do, they join the ranks of the heroes in our midst.

> \* *Peter Kissinger, President and CEO of the AAA Foundation, says that four people die in the United States each day in a traffic accidents caused by drivers who flees the scene of the accidents. From 2000 to 2009, hit-and-run drivers killed 16,382 people in the United States.*

# It's Not Goodbye

I AM THE youngest of six siblings by many years, and when I was a little fella, I hated going to the airport. When I was seven, my sister took an airplane to start her adult life in a place far away from our New York home. I said *goodbye* to her, and she left a sadder, quieter home. I hated goodbyes, and each year there were more. I was always glad to welcome folks to our airport, but I hated saying *goodbye*. I said *goodbye* to my oldest sister, my oldest brother, then to my other sister. Finally, I reached a point where I refused to say *goodbyes* any more. When anyone else would leave, I would hide to avoid saying *goodbye*.

When I was ten, my second brother got ready to move away from home to a faraway place. This time, he moved by car, and just before he left, he asked if he could talk to me. He told me that family would always be family and we never had to say goodbye. I replied, "Well, everyone still leaves, don't they?" He said, "Our family seems to be heading to California, so we're leaving, but we'll come back. We're all heading to California, and some day you will too." Then he said, "You never have to say *goodbye*, just say *so long. I* asked, "Instead of goodbye, *so long?* " He said, "It's *always so long until we meet again."* As he and his wife drove out the driveway, I called out, "Hey Rob, so long and thank you!"

When I was eighteen, I finally joined my family in California. Sadly, soon after I arrived in California, my brother, Rob, found out he would not be staying there long. After long months of severe pain, he was told by his doctor that he was terminally ill, and had at most three months to live. To make things worse, his cancer was so rare that they only knew of one other person who had ever had it. He was twenty six, and was to live just four months more.

Was this *goodbye*? I hardly knew how to say *goodbye*, I had just come to say "we meet again."

A month before my brother died, I shook his hand and a tear rolled down my cheek. I said "Rob, I don't want to say *goodbye*." He looked at me, hugged me, and smiled. He said "Don't say *goodbye*, say *so long.....until we meet again.*"

Over the years I have had a little niece, two parents, my best friend, and others who mean so much to me, all enter into eternity, and I have not said *goodbye* to any of them; it was always "So long." Today, my daughter at age eighteen, flew away from my home in Georgia to start her adult life in Washington State. My heart was heavy as I faced her going so far away, because even years later, I still hated saying *goodbye*. I looked at her just before she entered the Hartsfield Jackson Airport in Atlanta, Georgia, and called out to her, "So long.....until we meet again. My little girl, all grown up." As she walked through the airport doors, I thought of my brother was glad for when he told me, "It's not goodbye, it's till we meet again."

Those left behind are rarely thought of as heroes, but heroes are people who are looked up to for doing something noble. Accepting the need to let go and the act of letting go is a noble act in itself. At every airport and bus terminal there are heroes letting go. We are in the midst of heroes; all we have to do is to look for them, even in the airports.

# AFTER ANDY

ANDY WAS TWELVE years old. He was a child every parent would've loved to have. He put his all into everything he did. Though, like most children, he had his ups and downs. He loved school and excelled in every class, though he did not enjoy math as much as his other classes. He was a good athlete in baseball and Tai Kwan Do. His middle school baseball coach said that he was the best short stop that he had coached in his twenty-two years of coaching.

He enjoyed volunteering at a nursing home near where he lived. There, he read and listened to the stories of many of the men and women. He reached out to those who were disabled and came to the aid of anyone he thought was being bullied. He took it upon himself to look out after his family, even away from their home. If someone remotely threatened his brother or sisters, they had Andy to face. He wasn't mean, he was just fearless when it came to looking out after his family.

He wasn't perfect, but his weaknesses were age appropriate. He sometimes had his room a mess and enjoyed teasing his brother and two sisters regularly. He wasn't always neat or clean, and would even wipe his hands on his shirt or pants while playing or working outside. Every once in a while, he would need directions repeated more than once by his parents, but for the most part, he had a relaxed and easy going personality. He had a temper that could get hot, though it rarely did.

Andy was excited, because he just had his braces taken off. He and his mother had just left the Orthodontist and were driving home. His mother was going to stop off at an Ice Cream Store to celebrate by eating something really gooey, the kind of food he couldn't eat when he had his braces on. They were one block from the Ice Cream Store and the light for Andy's mother had turned green. As she had done thousands of times before, she entered the intersection at a safe speed driving carefully. A logging truck coming from a side street, traveling a lot faster than it should have been, with the driver texting another trucker went through the intersection against the red light. His truck hit Andy's car, and the point of impact was where Andy was sitting. As the metal began to twist around Andy, he had time to call out to his mother, "I love you!"

After the impact and dust settled, the truck was on top of the car Andy was in. Andy and his mother were pinned in the car. His mother's arms were pinned and the airbags had deflated on top of her legs, making it so she couldn't move her arms or her legs more than a few inches. She could feel something wet on the side of her face. She called out, "Andy, are you alright?" Andy didn't answer. She could see him but he didn't seem to be moving. She called to him again, still no answer. She thought, "Dear God, don't let my baby be dead." As she thought on it, she became aware of people outside the car trying to help get them out. Just as she focused on her rescuers, everything went black.

Andy's mother woke up in a strange bed with tubes sticking out of her right arm, which had extra support. Her right leg was in a cast. It took a few minutes for her eyes to focus, but when she was able, she saw three of her four children standing at the foot of the bed. Her parents and her husband's parents were standing behind her children. Before she saw, she felt her husband standing next to her by her right arm. There was someone who she didn't know standing on the other side of her, across from her husband. He looked like a doctor or nurse. She noticed everyone, but the doctor or nurse, looked like they had been crying.

As soon as she could talk she asked, "Where is Andy?" Her husband gently stroked her hair while his eyes filled with tears, but he didn't say anything. She repeated her question, "I asked a question, where is Andy?" The man who looked like a doctor, who was in fact a doctor, spoke for the first time. He said, "I'm Dr. Strong. We will answer your question, but I need to find out how you are doing first. To do that, I will just need to ask you a few questions." "I'm fine, tell me where Andy is," she said.

Dr. Strong said, "First, the questions." Andy's mother reluctantly agreed. Dr. Strong asked the first question, "What is your full name?" Andy's mother replied, "Deborah Renee Killian." He asked the next question, "Who is the man standing across from me?" Deborah responded quickly, "My husband, Teddy Killian." Dr. Strong asked the third question, "Who are the young people at the end of your bed?" Deborah, even more quickly replied, "They are three of my four children, Amy, Aileen, and Allan. Andy is my son who is not here. The people standing behind them are my parents and my in laws. Any other questions you have for me? I've had enough of this. Tell me where Andy is." Dr. Strong said, "Just two more questions, what day is it today?" Deborah said, "Thursday March 20th." Dr. Strong said, "It was Thursday when your accident occurred. Today is Friday March 21st. One last question, what is your street address?" Deborah said, "1881 Sycamore Canyon Road, now where is my son?"

Dr. Strong looked at Teddy, Teddy nodded. He gently said in a quiet voice, "Honey, Andy passed away when the truck hit you. He was gone instantly." Deborah lost all color. Her eyes became lifeless as soon as she heard her husband. Deborah yelled, "No!" She took a deep breath and became quiet. Her tears would fall later.

Telling Deborah that her oldest son had died was the last thing Teddy wanted to do. When he first heard that Andy had died and his wife was seriously hurt, a part of Teddy had died. Knowing that Deborah was going to be okay brought a ray of hope to his heart, which was quickly doused when he told his wife what she didn't want to hear but knew with in her heart. If she didn't, why did she ask so many times and in such an insistent way? As he told her what she didn't want to hear, he watched her usual sparkle fade away lost in her grief. He watched her quiet turn into grief that came to the surface in the form of tears. He stood helplessly watching her as she was lost in her tears, wanting to reach out to her but he just didn't know how.

Teddy saw a change in Deborah's eyes and her tears stopped. She said suddenly said, "I need to get out this hospital bed so I can help with Andy's funeral arrangements." Teddy at a near whisper said, "I've already made them." Deborah sat bolt upright and said, "No, no, no, my baby just died. I will not be left out of his last moments on earth. I know his favorite color, I know his favorite shirt, and I know his favorite hymns. I know what he loves. He was a part of me I need to be a part of his funeral. No hospital bed, no injury, or doctor is going to keep me from this." Deborah looked at Dr. Strong and said, "You have exactly one hundred twenty minutes to take care of the paper work to release me from your hospital, or I will leave on my own, even without your release." She turned to Teddy and said, "If you choose not to drive me home, unless Dr. Strong releases me, then I will call a taxi and go home on my own." She turned back to the doctor and said, "I need my clothes and all of these tubes out of me." No one was sure what to do. Deborah had never talked like this before. Deborah looked at the doctor and said, "What are you standing around for? Time is wasting. You have just one hundred sixteen minutes left."

One hundred ten minutes later, Deborah was released from the hospital even though her doctor didn't think it was the wisest thing for her to do, but he was too wise to tell her that. For the next few days there was so much going on with the funeral, greeting family and friends while looking after the rest of her children, husband, parents, and in laws for her to focus on her grief or her own health. Deborah buried her grief for short periods of time by cooking, baking, cleaning, and visiting. During visiting hours at the funeral home, Deborah couldn't stop looking at Andy. She wanted to keep the image of his last moments on earth burned into her memory for as long as she lived. During the days of the funeral, from deep within her broken heart, a flood of tears came out that never stopped.

There came a day when there was no more tears to fall, but her broken heart would remain the same forever.

Teddy was a man's man. He was raised to never show tears, but his little boy had just died. His son was gone forever and his wife was severely injured, though she would not allow herself to feel the hurt of her injury. Like Deborah, Teddy's heart was broken. For the benefit of his other children, his parents, his in laws, and friends who came to support their family as they grieved, Teddy was bigger than life. He frequently checked on everyone making sure they were doing as well as they could under the circumstance, joked and told stories. When he was alone late at night he cried with unashamed tears, but no matter how much he cried, it didn't take away the hurt he felt deep within his heart. The hurt would stay with Teddy as long as he lived. Andy was a part of Teddy that death could not take away.

Amy, Aileen, and Allen were overwhelmed by all of the activities surrounding Andy's funeral. They were just beginning to miss their brother and their protector. The full impact of Andy's passing would not hit them until after the funeral, days and months after. They would reach a time when they would long to hear Andy's laughter and have his protection from bullies and people who had over inflated egos. As each day passed without Andy, his memory didn't fade. Every day would bring moments when each of them would give everything they held dear to be teased by Andy, just one more time. Amy, Aileen and Allen would have an ache for their brother for the rest of their lives.

For Andy's grandparents, they too loved him and grieved for him, but somehow, Andy's death made the sunset of their lives seem easier to face. Still, they hurt. They all felt like they should never see their children or grandchildren's lives come to a close, they were supposed to die first. The thought of this increased their grief.

After the last person left the grave side service, there were still some of their good friends who would check on Teddy and Deborah's family to encourage them, but after four or five months, even that stopped. As for Teddy and Deborah, their grief never ended. For Deborah, some days she hurt so badly she didn't want to get out of bed, but her family needed her. In spite of her pain, she learned the hard lesson of living without her Andy. For Teddy, the ache in his heart would hit him hard when he least expected it. For example, when he was telling a story, passing by a landmark that he and Andy enjoyed seeing, or even when he was eating a favorite food that Andy enjoyed as well.

Fourteen months after Andy was killed, the truck driver who killed him was found guilty of involuntary manslaughter. He was sentenced to ten years but could get out in five. Not only had the truck driver been on the cell phone when he hit Deborah and Andy, he was also driving at a high rate of speed, failed to stop at a stop light, and was driving under the influence of an illegal drug. The truck driver's family was very upset that he was to spend ten years, more or less, in jail and complained bitterly to the press. The press asked Teddy how he felt about the sentence. He said, "Ten years in jail is a long time, but this man, by doing what he did, sentenced my family to life without Andy. Which sentence is longer?"

When a child dies, it is a tragedy. When a child dies who doesn't have to, that is more than a tragedy, and it is a tragedy that didn't have to happen. For children, the leading cause of deaths is car accidents. Children, age twelve and older, are more likely to be killed in car accidents than younger children. *There is an average of three children every day who are killed in car accidents, according to KidsandCars. org.*

Twenty-two heroes are created every day because of children who die in car wrecks. Heroes, innocent victims who survive and help others survive children torn from their lives. We walk among these heroes never knowing, because we aren't looking for them. We are in the midst of heroes; all we have to do is to look for them.

# CANCER

# Because Of Cancer

CHUCK IS FORTY-THREE years old. Five years ago he had a perfect life or as perfect as any man should have. He was a vice president of a startup computer software business. He had been married for fourteen years to a beautiful intelligent woman named Jane. He called her Plain Jane. She was anything but plain. She had a quiet beauty and a way of making anyone around her feel her feel totally at ease. Her kindness and warmth was well known. Chuck and Jane had three beautiful children, a twelve year old girl named Angela and identical ten year old twin boys named Peter and Patrick.

Chuck is a real family man. He and his wife go out for special "just the two of them" nights twice a month to a movie, dinner or a moon light walk. He and his wife are soccer parents, recreational league football parents and PTO parents. He is a Cub Scout leader while Jane is a Girl Scout mom. He makes time to go camping, fishing, and hunting as well as to museums and amusement parks together regularly. As a family they kayak together in some of the most scenic though quite rivers and streams that they can find.

Chuck enjoys sports of any kind, watches some but is active in many. He plays tennis and basketball with his family of course. He doesn't like running but it keeps him healthy so he runs two miles per day four days a week. Until five years ago he rarely had even a sniffle or cold. He wasn't always healthy. When he met his wife he was a two pack a day cigarette smoker, drank enough beer to get drunk on a regular basis. He seemed to always have at least one joint to light up and a couple more to share with his friends.

Chuck was in grad school when he met Jane. He was

likeable enough to have no shortage of women to be with but none like Jane. By the time he had five dates with her he knew he wanted to marry her. When he first asked her to marry him she told him no because she just couldn't stand the thought of being married to a smoker. In fact she told him that he could not kiss her again until he stopped smoking as she hated the taste of a smoky kiss.

Chuck was angry when Jane gave him the choice between smoking or her. He had smoked since he was cigarettes since he was thirteen. He had smoked for ten years and really enjoyed smoking. Why should he let a girl make him quit something he truly loved doing? She was a girl who he would do anything for. If she had asked him to go get some edelweiss whatever that is he would drop everything and climb to the tops of the Swiss Alps to find it if he knew what it looked like. Quitting smoking was so much harder than climbing the Alps. He always said he could quit smoking any time he wanted to. He wanted to so badly but it was so hard. He used a patch and anti nicotine gum but for the first month it still was a minute by minute effort. Without thinking about it he also quit smoking pot and drinking too much. When Jane knew he quit smoking she also knew he had quit pot and overdrinking. Chuck knew that after she asked him to kiss her for the first time since she had told him that she wouldn't marry him. The kiss was one Chuck would remember the rest of his life because after the kiss Jane said one word, "Yes". He was already walking on air when Jane added, "You know what really convinces me to marry you is that you also quit using pot and getting drunk."

For fourteen years life was as good as it gets but then just as it felt as if Chuck had arrived he began to cough a lot and more and more when he coughed he coughed up blood, not a lot but some. He developed a hoarseness that at first seemed like part of a cold he had but after the cold went away the hoarseness did not. It started to hurt to breathe. His father had died of leukemia when he was ten. He remembered how much pain his father was in the last months of his life. He was afraid that he had cancer just like his father had. His father was the same age as Chuck when he died. Chuck didn't want to tell Jane about what was happening to him. It wasn't that he was afraid to show her how afraid he was, he just didn't want her to worry.

Finally he was worried enough to talk to Jane about it. He told her that he would have talked to her sooner but he didn't want her to worry. Jane said, "Of course I am concerned but I won't worry until I know that there is something to worry about. With Jane by his side he saw a doctor and explained his symptoms. His doctor told him that what he described was serious but that tests would need to be done to know for certain. Chest X-rays were taken, a CAT scan was done as well as an MRI. After a few days his doctor called them and asked them to come in to his office. He told Chad he had stage two lung cancer. He told him that treatment needed to be begun soon. He recommended that the treatment be surgery to remove the tumor, chemotherapy and radiation. He needed permission to schedule surgery. Chuck told him he would call by the end of the day. Chuck was overwhelmed by the diagnosis. He couldn't look up for a few minutes. When he did he saw Jane crying silently, keeping a tight hold on his hand.

Chuck couldn't say a word on the way home. He and Jane had a deep faith in the God above but having a death sentence thrown at him was a blow. At first he was angry, at whom he wasn't sure, probably more at himself for smoking all of those years but angry at a lot of things. This wasn't fair. Life was good. His family needed him. Didn't God understand that? He allowed himself some time for self-pity but since he was a man who didn't like to waste time and self-pity was a waste of time he didn't feel sorry for himself very long. He decided that if he was going to beat the cancer that had such a hold on him he was going to have to know as about it as he could.

As soon as he could get on his computer he looked up stage two lung cancer. Chuck found out some facts that were very disturbing to him. According to the National Cancer Institution about 220,000 people in the United

States are diagnosed with lung cancer each year and that about 157,000 people will die from it. The five year survival rate was only about fifteen percent. He didn't like what he found out. He felt like the odds were against him. He did not want to have surgery, chemo or radiation because of the memories of the horrors his father went through but no matter how hard he looked these treatments were the only ones that could site statistically any survival rate.

He looked in to alternative ways that his cancer could be treated. There were a lot of promises but mot a lot of data to back up the promises as viable treatment plans. He needed a sure thing that had at least some successes. He thought that maybe after he tried the more traditional plans that had at least a bit of a proven track record and still hadn't beaten his lung cancer then he would look in to the alternate approaches.

Chuck had been so focused on his research that he lost track of time. All he knew was that he must have been on his computer for hours. It was long enough for him to not know where his wife was and he needed to talk to her. He turned off the computer and looked for his wife. He found Jane in their bedroom. She was on her knees by the side of her bed. He told her that he was going to call the doctor and tell him to schedule surgery. They both cried.

Chuck called his doctor to tell give him permission to schedule surgery. An hour after Chuck called his doctor the doctor called him back and told him surgery was scheduled in five days. His doctor said, "If all goes well, Chemo therapy which was a chemical cocktail designed to kill living cells cancer and healthy cells together would start ten days later and radiation soon after. I know that you are aware of the low survival percentages are but you have some things in your favor. You quit smoking ten years earlier, you are a strong young man and you have a good attitude. The biggest thing is your attitude. If you think you will die you will but if you fight your cancer with all of your heart there is something about attitude that makes a real difference."

Jane told Chuck that you are not fighting this alone.

Our faith will keep you, I am beside you and when we tell our children as gently as we can they will be with you too. Chuck asked Jane, Do we have to?" Jane said, "Yes we do because we are a family...for good and bad. Besides you never know this could be good." That evening after dinner Chuck and Jane told their children that Chuck was very sick that in about a week he would be going to the hospital for surgery and after surgery would be going there quite a lot. The children learned that Chuck had cancer and that they would need to be closer as a family than they ever were before. Angela asked Chuck if they should worry. Chuck said, "Baby it's not time to worry. Mom will let you know when it's time to worry but it's always a good idea to get help from above."

Chuck visited with his boss the next day and explained why he would need to take time off. His boss was his friend and so was deeply concerned. He wanted to help Chuck so much so that he canceled meetings and rescheduled a business trip to be at the hospital when Chuck had his surgery and made arrangements for Chuck's work to be taken care of until he was back on his feet again. Five days later Chuck entered the hospital for what would become the hardest days of his life. Surgery made him sore as he knew it would but recovery went along fairly smoothly. Chemo therapy was very hard on him causing his hair to fall out, severe nausea, bad vomiting and extreme fatigue. His radiation therapy wasn't as bad but he developed a dry cough and difficulty swallowing. Chuck lost a great deal of weight. Six weeks after Chuck's last radiation treatment he went back to the oncologist who did extensive tests and did not find any indication that he had any more cancer cells left in his body. Chuck and his family breathed a sigh of relief for the moment. He was to return for follow up checkups every 3 months for the next three years and then twice a year for the following two years. The waiting was to be almost as hard as the cancer. In the next five years his dreams and the dreams of Jane were too often invaded by dreams of his cancer coming back.

After Chuck's bout with self-pity he never let himself

feel self-pity again. To him the lung cancer was a personal enemy and he aced it like a soldier on the front lines. He tried very hard to be upbeat and positive around Jane, Angela, Peter and Patrick. When he felt the most ill and could hardly lift his head, when it seemed as though the cure was worse than the disease, he waited until everyone including Jane was asleep before he allowed himself the luxury of feeling discouraged. He felt that if he was to beat lung cancer he could not afford to spend time being discouraged for very long. It was at those times he turned towards spirituality.

Coming face to face with his own mortality made Chuck a better man. He had always enjoyed time spent with his family before he had cancer but after he had cancer he enjoyed time spent with them even more. He always worked hard at his job before he had cancer but after he had cancer he found ways to put more in to his job. He found ways to do his job better limiting the time he spent with his family, his community and his friends. He and Jane always were deeply in love before Chuck had cancer but after he had cancer their moments together were more precious. He was always an honorable man before he had cancer but because he was so focused on spending the moments of his life well after he had cancer he was even a more honorable after he had cancer. Chuck proved to be among the lucky fifteen percent who survived more than five years and he never forgot the lessons he learned from the war of his life.

A hero is one who has great courage. Chuck was one such man. Every year there more people who are fighting a war with cancer. It is a war that still has a high fatality rate. In spite of the number of fatalities, those heroes who are fighting cancer fight with great courage and grace. It is estimated that there are about twelve million heroes fighting cancer in the United States. We are in the midst of heroes we just have to look for them.

# In Support Of a Fighter

JANE IS A beautiful and intelligent woman. She is married to a man named Chuck. She is a realtor, and a mother of three children. Up until about six years ago, she had a perfect life, or as close to perfect as anyone could have. Jane and Chuck had been married for fourteen years, and she adored her husband. They had pet names for each other; she called him Chuck Chuck, and he called her Plain Jane. She thought he was the kindest and best looking man alive. She had a quiet beauty, and a way of making everyone around her feel at ease. Her kindness and warmth was well known, and Jane's personality made her a great part time realtor, a career she could do while her children were in school.

Chuck and Jane had three beautiful children, a twelve year old girl named Angela, and identical ten year old fraternal twin boys, named Peter and Patrick. Jane was a good mother who was active in her young children's lives. She was a soccer mom, a classroom mother, and a Girl Scout mom. In addition, she was a PTO and recreational league parent. The children were well adjusted and happy, each of them being well liked by their peers and adults.

Angela was already growing to be a beautiful young lady, and was incredibly intelligent. She was allowed to skip a grade and was in the gifted program in Middle School. Her favorite subjects were math and science. She wanted to either be a doctor or a bio medical engineer when she grew up. Angela was a Girl Scout focusing on getting her Girl Scout Gold Award. She also was involved in any kind of athletics, especially soccer. She loved playing basketball, fishing, hunting, and kayaking with her family.

Peter and Patrick were active young boys who liked

taking things apart and finding out why they worked. They liked to build things even more than they liked taking them apart. Like their sister, they did well in school. They were both in the gifted program and enjoyed athletics even more than Angela. They were active in neighborhood baseball, recreational league football, and cub scouting, where they both built and raced their own Pinewood Derby cars. Like their sister, they enjoyed playing basketball, going camping, kayaking, fishing, and hunting with their family.

Chuck, Jane, Angela, Peter, and Patrick were members of an ideal family. They were a family that so many other families wanted to be like. It seemed like they were a family that always avoided any major conflicts or problems. For a while there weren't any problems, until Chuck came down with a cold he couldn't seem to shake. She noticed that he had a dry cough that continued to get worse. Along with the cough, Chuck developed a hoarseness that would not go away. Jane knew that he was worried, but he wouldn't tell her anything. She wasn't supposed to know, but she loved Chuck and noticed everything about him. When he began to cough up blood and breathing began to hurt, Chuck approached Jane and told her that he needed to see a doctor; so they went together.

His doctor ran a number of tests on Chuck and x-rayed his chest. Then he sent him to an oncologist, a cancer specialist. The oncologist ran more tests, and within a few days, his oncologist called them in to see him. He told them that Chuck had stage two lung cancer. This was devastating news for both Chuck and Jane. The doctor recommended that the course of treatment be surgery to remove the tumor, chemotherapy, and radiation, but first he needed permission to schedule the surgery. Chuck didn't look up for a few minutes, and Jane began to silently cry. When Chuck looked up, he saw the doctor waiting for an answer from him and Jane's tears falling as she held tightly to his hand. In a daze, he told the doctor that he would call him by the end of the day to let him know if he wanted surgery or not.

Chuck couldn't say a word on the way home. Jane sat quietly next to him wanting to reach out, but knowing that this was not the time, so she hoped her love and support for him could be felt in his moment of grief. As soon as they got home, Chuck immediately got on his computer to find out what he could about lung cancer. Jane desperately wanted Chuck to agree to the treatment plan his oncologist proposed as soon as he could, but she knew it wasn't up to her, it was up to Chuck. Jane sought out comfort and solace in her room beside the bed on her knees. This is where Chuck found her when he finished his research and made the decision that he would follow his doctor's recommended cancer treatment plan. He told his wife what he had in mind and that he was ready to call his doctor to ask him to schedule surgery as soon as possible. They both cried.

Chuck called his doctor to tell give him permission to schedule surgery, and within an hour, the doctor called him back and told him surgery was scheduled in five days.

Jane told Chuck, "You aren't fighting this alone. Our faith will keep you, I am beside you. When we tell our children as gently as we can, they will be with you too." Chuck asked, "Do we have to?" Jane said, "Yes, we do, because we are a family...through the good and bad. Besides, you never know, this *could* be good." That evening after dinner, Chuck and Jane told their children that Chuck was very sick and that in about a week he would be going to the hospital for surgery, and after surgery he would be going there quite frequently. The children learned that Chuck had cancer and that they would need to be closer as a family than they ever were before. Angela asked her dad if they should worry, and Chuck said, "Baby, it's not time to worry. Mom will let you know when it's time to worry, but it's always a good idea to get help from above."

The cancer that Chuck was to fight for the next five years would effectively change everyone in his family for the rest of their lives. It would bring an already close family closer, as only hard fought battles can do. Chuck's side effects to his treatment were nausea, loss of energy, fatigue, a bad cough, and sore throat. So, the rest of the family had to help out doing many of the things that Chuck did to keep the family doing well.

Without hurting Chuck's feelings, Jane took charge of running the family, especially when Chuck was at his weakest. She made sure every bill was paid on time and that any well-wisher who contacted the family via internet, snail mail, or in person was thanked, and monitored and limited visits when he wasn't able stand much. As the emails, messages, and letters of encouragement came in along with any flowers and gifts, she shared them with Chuck, her children, and their parents. She took over as many of the family man duties that Chuck did as she could without stopping the Mom duties she always did. When she went bed, she slept in cat naps, watching over Chuck when he was at home; and beside him the many days he spent in the hospital. Jane was the person that everyone went to as a sounding board, because she had a word in season for everyone. She found those words by spending as much time as she could on her knees. When she needed to cry, which was often, she waited until everyone was asleep. She rarely had time for herself and when she did, she felt guilty for taking the time. Until Chuck had cancer, Jane never knew how much time she had wasted, but after his cancer she put more time into her day.

When Chuck started spending so much time at the hospital, Angela went with him as often as she could. She saw so many people who were ill or hurt, and she was determined to one day become a doctor to help people like the ones she saw. Whenever anyone came near her that worked in the hospital, including custodians and kitchen help, she asked them as many questions as she dared. She went out of her way to help her over worked and exhausted mother. She tried hard to be the perfect daughter, not wanting to add to her parents' already full plate. Sometimes, the stress of trying so hard caused her to break down in tears or blow up at her brothers, which resulted in fleeing to her mother for comfort. She became more focused on her school work, kept up all of her outside of school activities as best as she could, looked out after her brothers when they would let her, and even let them tease her. Although she didn't like to be teased, she understood that it was their way to release some of their stress and worry over their dad.

Chuck's cancer effected Peter and Patrick more than anyone else in his family. The boys went from being secure little boys, who knew that their mom and dad could do anything, to not being so sure about anything. For many months after their dad became ill, he was too sick, weak, and tired to do much of anything with them. Until their dad became ill, Patrick and Peter had not been exposed to many people who were ill and didn't even know of many who had died. After their dad had cancer, they had firsthand knowledge of their very ill father. They learned about death by seeing patients in various stages of cancer, fighting at the hospital that their dad was at. By seeing this, day after day, they feared that their dad would die and the thought haunted them. Their grades were never as good as their sister's, but they had been slacking since their father fell ill. When their mother realized, she had a talk with them. She told them that their father was fighting cancer as hard as he could, but if they would work hard to do well in school, in spite of their fears, it would help their dad. As they heard these words, they made it their mission to work hard and put every ounce of effort into not only school, but the other activities they participated in. Still, their dad's illness shook their self-confidence and openness. Their strength was working with their hands, so they spent more time with their grandfather, a builder, and learned to create beautiful woodwork.

Chuck's determination and courage, that finally allowed him victory over a terrible enemy, inspired everyone who knew him, especially his family, to be determined putting forth real effort in everything they did. He often said the support he received from his family and their effort gave him courage to keep fighting when he thought he had none. The love that his parents, in laws, wife, and children gave to him and to each other helped him stay focused on the task at hand.

The cancer was a terrifying enemy, but along the way, they all learned lessons that could've only been taught by facing such an adversary; the importance of making the most of every moment, the fact that tomorrow is not guaranteed, the strength that love can bring, the value of sharing how much the ones you love mean to you, and the value of a word in season.

Heroes are people who display courage and the will for self-sacrifice, and Chuck's family did just that. Over eleven million Americans are either going through cancer treatment currently, or have in the past. They have at least two family members supporting them per cancer survivor, making it possible for there to be at least twenty-two million people/heroes who are supporting heroes who are fighting or have fought cancer and won. We are in the midst of heroes, even heroes in blue jeans, we just have to look for them.

# Keep On Fighting

GINNY IS SEVEN and a half years old, and in the hospital again. She has leukemia, and this is the second time that she has to fight this terrible cancer. This time, she is convinced that she will beat the cancer once and for all.

The first time she had leukemia, she was just three and a half years old. Until Ginny was sick, she was a bubbly, happy little girl. When she got sick, no one really knew at first. She just stopped feeling like running, jumping, or even smiling much. She only wanted to sleep or cuddle up with her favorite dolly.

Ginny's mother and father noticed her change in behavior; she'd been so full of energy only the day before they thought that she had the flu. They made sure she had enough to drink and tried to encourage her to eat at least a little. Her mother showered her with love and checked on her frequently, reading to her and singing her favorite songs. Her mother became concerned when Ginny's health didn't improve three days later. Her father had begun to worry too, but wasn't willing to say so or to share his fear with his wife, scared that he might make things harder on her. Instead, he kept saying that it was just the flu and Ginny would feel better soon. He suggested that if Ginny wasn't feeling better in a day or two, they'd take her to see the doctor, and her mother agreed.

In two days she hadn't changed, so they took her to see a pediatrician. When she arrived at the doctor's office, she saw lots of toys in the waiting room. She would have liked to have played with them, but she was just too tired. She saw her doctor and many important people in white coats that asked her lots of questions and poked her several times, and even though they were kind, they seemed sad for her.

After the doctors poked at Ginny and asked her questions, one man in a white coat asked to speak to her parents. Whatever he said made her mother cry and her father keep clearing his throat. Then, the room got quiet. Her father stood still with his hands in his pockets, looking as scared as Ginny felt. Her mother cried harder, but without any sound. Ginny didn't know what was going on, but she knew that the man in the white coat upset her parents and she didn't like that.

Ginny's mother reached out to her, and held her like she had when she was a baby. Her mother told Ginny that the man in the white coat was a doctor, a special doctor. They knew why she wasn't feeling well and could make her better, but she'd be sicker before she progressed. Ginny's sickness had two names, the first name was cancer and the other name was leukemia. This didn't make sense to Ginny but she trusted her mother.

Ginny's parents took her to the hospital to have what her father called "an operation". She didn't know what that meant, but she knew that she was more afraid than she'd ever been before. She didn't want to be at the hospital, where all the doctors poked her with needles and hooked her up to machines. As she cried, her mother held her as best as she could and cried with her.

Early the next morning, the doctors tried to wake her, only being partially successful. When she was fully alert, she realized she was on a new bed, one with wobbly wheels, and her father was stroking her hair, telling her that he loved her over and over. A nice lady in a uniform, with Winnie the Pooh pictures on it, told her good morning. Then, she gave her a stuffed animal kitten, knowing that she loved them. The nurse told her that she was going to give her something through the bag next to her arm that would make her go to sleep, and it was to make her feel better. She told Ginny that she wouldn't feel better right away, and she'd hurt after she woke up, but she'd get better soon. Ginny started to cry, and the nurse promised to stay with her the whole time, while she hugged her. Ginny went to sleep holding tightly to her kitty.

When she woke up, her pain was terrible, but her parents, along with the nurse with the Winnie the Pooh Uniform, was beside her bed and each of them told her how good she had done, which made her feel a little better. It took a little while, but Ginny almost got back to normal. She still was tired a lot, but she had begun to play a little. A month later, her parents took her back to the hospital, though she didn't want to go. She was poked at again and this time, some medicine from an ugly bag next to her was injected in her through a needle and tubes. It made her very sick, but she had to continue coming back and getting the treatments. She didn't like this at all, but still trusted her parents and the nurse with the Winnie the Pooh uniform.

After the third time Ginny had gone through chemo, all of her beautiful hair fell out in big clumps and she became bald. She loved her hair, but now it was all gone. She asked her mother if she was dying. Her mother told her she wasn't dying, but the medicine that was fighting her cancer sometimes made people's hair fall out, but it would grow back soon. Until it did, there were all kinds of pretty hats and wigs she could wear. Her father asked her how she would like it if his hair fell out too, to make her laugh. Ginny asked if he would take her medicine too. He quickly responded, "Oh no, my barber can take my hair off a lot easier." Her mother said, "My hair dresser can do the same thing for me, plus I can donate my hair to Locks of Love. They use hair like mine to make wigs for girls and ladies whose hair falls out like yours did. Maybe Locks of Love will have a wig for you to wear."

Within hours, both parents became bald, and when both sets of grandparents heard what her parents did, they did the same. Soon, many of her Aunts, Uncles, cousins and even some family friends donated their hair to Locks of Love. The unselfish act of becoming bald was an outward sign of their love for Ginny, and a show of support for Ginny in her battle against leukemia. It was this same love, laughter, and care that made it easier for her to feel better, to laugh, and smile. It made it possible for Ginny to be a Cancer survivor for forty-two months. Her hair grew back even prettier than before, and she greeted every new day with a smile, and made everyone who knew her smile too.

Six months ago, Ginny began to feel sick again. At first, she thought it was the flu, but the feeling of being ill would not go away. It took her a few days to let her parents know how she was feeling. As each day passed, Ginny began to feel more and more like she felt when she was little; when the doctor's told her she had cancer. As soon as she told her parents, they immediately scheduled an appointment with her oncologist.

On the way to the doctor's, Ginny said to her mother, "Last night, I dreamed that I died. I can't remember anything that I saw, only how I felt. I felt so much love and safety. It was such a wonderful feeling that I didn't want to leave, but then I saw you, daddy and little sis crying by my body. Then I knew I didn't want to go yet. Mommy, I am not afraid to die. I just don't want to yet. I know my leukemia has come back." Her mother, with tears rolling down her cheeks, said, "I think you are right. Your cancer has come back, but you have to fight it. I won't let you give up, and I don't want you to go. You just have to fight it."

What Ginny and her mother feared was confirmed by her doctor, just two days later. Plans for fighting her cancer were made; and this time surgery would not be part of the battle plan, but chemotherapy and radiation therapy was. Ginny was relieved by not having to go through surgery again, but she was terrified of the thought of having to go through chemotherapy again, remembering how she lost all of her hair. She loved her hair even more now, and the thought of losing it brought her to tears for the first time. They freely fell, wave after wave of overwhelming despair hit her, and her mother joined.

Her father came into the office, just as Ginny and her mother felt the worst. Ginny looked over at her father and noticed that he had a black eye. She said, "Daddy, what is wrong with your eye? You look like my best friend Timmy, after he got in a fight by a big boy." Her father said, "I was in such a hurry to get here that when I got out of the car, I forgot to open the door all the way and it hit my eye on my way out. My eye hurts a lot, but not as much as my heart does for you to have to face the fight of your life. You beat leukemia once you can do it again, but only if you fight it." As Ginny's mother looked on and listened to her husband, she had an idea.

Ginny's first chemotherapy procedure was scheduled in two weeks. Her mother first talked to her father to tell him her idea, which he thought was great. They both made a few phone calls and she talked to Ginny's elementary school principal, as he thought it was also a great idea.

The day before Ginny was to have her procedure done, Ginny's mother overslept. For some reason, her mother moved extra slow in everything she did, even the drive to school was unusually slow. They arrived at school almost two hours late, and as they pulled into the parking lot, Ginny's father pulled in right behind them. Ginny asked her father what he was doing there, and he told her he saw their car and wanted to go see her classroom with her, her mother, and little sis. Ginny said, "Daddy, did you bump your eye again? It's black." Her daddy laughed and said, "Getting to be a habit for me." Ginny laughed too, but just as they were entering the school, Ginny looked at her daddy again and said, "Your eye isn't hurt, it looks like you colored it. " Her mommy said, "Before we go any further, little Sis and I need to use the restroom, do you know where one is?" Ginny pointed at the nearest one.

Ginny's mother and little Sis weren't gone long, but when they came out, they too had black eyes. Ginny said, "What is going on?" "The answer to that is in the gym," Ginny's father said. He took Ginny's left hand and her mother took her right hand, and they walked to the gym. Before they entered, Ginny could hear a lot of voices. She would have held back if her parents weren't moving her forward. As they entered, the fifth grade band started playing. Ginny looked at the gym that was full of more people than she'd ever seen, and everyone in the gym had a black eye. There were so many signs all directed at her.

Some of the signs Ginny read were, "Keep fighting, Ginny," "Don't give up Ginny," "We Love you, Ginny" and "Don't Stop Fighting, Ginny." Everyone was chanting something that at first she didn't understand, which turned out to be, "Keep fighting, Ginny. Don't give up." All of these people, students, teachers, friends, and so many she didn't know, all of them in that gym wanted her to fight her leukemia. All of those people reaching out to her. She felt renewed courage and strength. She shed tears along with her parents, but they were tears of gratitude, not tears of fear. When she left the gym, she was ready to fight.

Just before the nurses put the bag of medicine above her arm, the nurse who was with her the first time, still wearing a uniform with Winnie the Pooh pictures on it, did something to her eye. She brought her a mirror and said, "Heard about all the black eyes in your neighborhood, thought you might want one too." *

Heroes are both male and female, with no limit on age. Heroes inspire us by their courage and their attitude to rise above everything. Cancer has a way of bringing out the hero in a person. Heroes, like Ginny, are all around us. In fact, we are in the midst of heroes.

* *The term leukemia refers to cancer of the white blood cells. Because their infection-fighting white blood cells are defective, children with leukemia may experience increased episodes of fevers and infections, pain in their bones, and fatigue.*

* *Leukemia affects about nine in one hundred thousand people each year. About twenty-two thousand people will die from leukemia each year. There is only about a forty-two percent five year survival rate. Adults are ten times more likely to develop leukemia than children. About five hundred children in the United States will die each year. Children under the age of four have a greater chance of developing leukemia than older children do.*

# FIGHTING A LOSING BATTLE

IT HAS BEEN said that life is a series of battles, some won and some lost. The battles of life begin when we take our first breath and end when we take our last one. Some battles are easier than others, while other battles were never meant for us to win. To those who choose to fight each battle with a will to win, even when they lose, they win. Long after battles that they lose, especially the final battle, they are remembered as winners.

At age sixty-three, Rose began the fight of her life. Six weeks before she began her fight, at her birthday party Rose shared with her family and friends, she felt like her life had been wonderful. She was a southern belle, born and bred. Her daddy was an attorney and a pecan farmer. Her Mama did not have a cash money job; instead, she worked hard at raising Rosie and her older sister to be true southern ladies and taking care of their home.

Rose shared her mother's love for flowers, music, fine arts, and the written word. As much as she loved those things, she enjoyed sharing her love of those things with other people, especially children. Rose grew up to be an accomplished pianist, locally known oil painter, expert gardener, and High School English teacher.

She was hired for her first teaching assignment at the same High school that she had attended. One of the teachers, who was hired at the same time as Rose, was a tall handsome dark haired Chemistry teacher. His name was Thomas. He was a true southern gentleman, quiet but strong. He was one of the most kind and caring men she had ever known. The more she got to know him, the better she liked him. He, in turn, was captivated by her beauty, sense of humor, and talent. He noticed how quickly her students grew to love her. The staff at school quickly loved her as well. He became her chief admirer. By the end of the school year, they were inseparable. By spring of their second year of teaching, they began a marriage that was to last forty-one years.

About a year into Thomas and Rose's marriage, Thomas quit teaching to start a landscaping business, and Rose had her first baby. Her baby's name was Olivia and two years later, s/he had her second baby, Abigail. For the next eight years, Rose focused on being a new mother and a book keeper for her husband's new business. She was an active member in a local Community Civic Organization and a campaign manager for her husband when he ran for election and reelection as a County Supervisor. After eight years of being home, Rose found herself missing teaching high school aged children, her love of books, and the joys of writing. She was offered a teaching position at the same high school that she had left.

During the next twenty-seven years, Rose hardly had any time to relax. She was not just a teacher to her one hundred-fifty students each year; she was a year book and debate team advisor, she was a department head, mentor teacher for new teachers, served on several committees, played organ and piano at her church and another church, served as chairwoman of her gardening club, was a girl scout leader, 4H leader, painted an average of twelve paintings each year, continued to be a book keeper for her husband's very successful business, active member of the chamber of commerce, and campaign chair for her husband's successful campaign for County supervisor every two years.

Rose was one of the most loved women in her area. She reached out to everyone and most returned her warmth. She had the ability to spot phony quickly, and didn't have time for anything or anyone who was not real or true. She gave her all to whatever she did in her work, to her family, and to her community. Nearing the end of her career, she noticed that it was harder to get her students to focus on what she loved to share. Her students had issues at home that she had no idea of how to help; drugs, violence, and indifference from parents and adults. She would never stop loving her students or the subject she taught, but it was time to retire. Her fellow teachers didn't want to see her go and felt her absence for years to come.

The first six months of her retirement were everything Rose had dreamed of. She and Thomas took a cruise they had talked about for years. She had never painted so well and her fall flowers had never looked so good. She had become the piano player and song leader for the Community Civic Organization that she belonged to, and spent time reading books that she had always promised that she would read when she had time. She spent time doing what she loved the best, being with her family and friends.

About six months after Rose began her retirement, her right breast became sore enough for her to see her doctor and old family friend. * As he examined her, it was not so much what he said that alarmed her, but the look he gave that made Rose very concerned. He told Rose that she could have nothing to worry about or it could be a lot to worry about. To be certain, he sent her to a specialist who ordered a diagnostic test or biopsy. She waited weeks to get the results and as she waited, her fears grew. Finally, she got word that she and Thomas needed to come see her doctor.

Upon arriving at the physician's office, they noticed that that her doctor had another doctor with him. He was an oncologist; a doctor who is a cancer specialist. He told her that she had inflammatory or stage III cancer in her right breast and that they found a smaller tumor or stage II cancer in her left breast.** Rose felt the floor crumble under her. She couldn't cry; she felt completely numb. For the first minute or two, she neither moved nor spoke. Thomas was almost as devastated. Rose was the love of his life. He had always thought that she would out live him, but this diagnosis was almost more than he could stand.

After a few minutes she said, "I will fight this." Her doctor said, "You can't fight it alone, but we as a team will fight it; you, your husband, your family, your doctors, nurses, and specialist." "Doctor, can we beat this cancer," Rose asked? Her doctor said, "Yes, if we fight it aggressively." He recommended that she have surgery to remove the cancer, either by lumpectomy (removing parts of her breasts where the cancer is) or mastectomy (removing all of her breast or breasts), but her surgeons would determine which would be the best procedure when they are doing the surgery. He said they should follow this up by chemo therapy and radiation. Thomas asked how soon that the surgery could be scheduled. The doctor said, "Within five days." Rose said, "Schedule it."

Rose did well in surgery. The surgeons did lumpectomies in both of her breasts and with more reconstruction necessary in her right breast than her left. For the next six months, Rose was very sick, losing her hair, along with a great deal of weight and energy while going through radiation and chemo. At her check up a week after her chemo and radiation, there was no cancer cells found. Rose and Thomas had the same good news at her annual exam, six months later.

For a few weeks after the checkup, Rose was busy with all the things she loved doing. One morning she woke up really hurting, but it eased up and eventually went away. However, in the days that followed, her pain came back lasting longer and being more intense each time. She was sure that her cancer had returned, but didn't want to share it with Thomas, knowing how upset he would be if he knew.

By the third week of pain, now so bad it was hard for her to sleep, she confided in her husband and scheduled an appointment with her doctor. He gave her a complete physical and ran diagnostic tests. Once again, it took a few weeks for the results to come back and they were negative. She was given some pain medicine and told her that it was probably nothing to worry about. Her pain grew, so she saw her doctor again five weeks later. He ran more tests and still the tests were negative. She was sure that she had cancer, but the doctor was missing it, so she scheduled an appointment with her oncologist. He ran extensive diagnostic tests and this time, he had news for Rose and Thomas that Rose had suspected all along.

Her Oncologist told her that her breast cancer had spread and they needed to do surgery as soon as possible. Rose gave her permission for the surgery to be done, but this surgery was harder on Rose and harder on her surgeons, because when they opened her up, the cancer had spread too much to for surgery to help. When Rose woke up, her doctor told her that they found out that she had stage four cancer. She was told that she was now fighting for her life. The weapons to fight the cancer would primarily be chemotherapy and radiation. Rose reached for her husband's hand and said, "I know it doesn't look good for me, but we will keep fighting this enemy and we will win."

Over the next eight months, Rose and her doctors fought hard using every weapon they had, even a couple of experimental ones. In addition to what the medical world gave her to fight her cancer, there were many fighting for her on their knees, offering prayers on her behalf, day and night. As she fought, the love that her community had for her came to her in waves; bringing food, flowers, gifts of all kinds, and reassurance of their support for her. Throughout her battle, Rose was always offering words of encouragement to others like, "Did you know that there are over two million survivors of breast cancer in the United States, and I am going to be two million and one?" As the battle raged, it was becoming more evident that Rose was losing her war against her evil foe. She continued to lose weight and her weariness increased as did her pain, in spite of the medication to ease that part of her battle.

For a long time, Thomas had believed that if Rose said she would beat her cancer she would. After a while, as he watched her lose ground to where it was only her will to live that kept her alive, he knew she wasn't going to win. How could she die? He needed her to live, as she was everything to him. He loved her more now than he had forty-one years ago. She couldn't go, they were supposed to spend their golden years together. How could he spend his golden years alone, without his best friend, his love?

Rose would not quit fighting, even as it was evident in her eyes that she knew the days left to battle were few. At the last doctor's visit, before she was to leave her home for the last time, her doctor told her that there was an experimental drug that might help Rose. He told her that she shouldn't get her hopes, but if she was willing to come to the hospital, he would administer it. She told her friend who visited her the next day that her doctor had found a miracle drug that would help her, and she was going to the hospital to get the drug the next day. She made it to the hospital, but within hours she slipped in to a coma, and within three days, slid into eternity. ***

It has been said that life is a series of battles, some won and some lost. The battles of life begin when we take our first breath and end when we take our last. Some battles are easier than others, while other battles were never meant for us to win. To those who choose to fight each battle with a will to win, even when they lose, they win. Long after battles that they lose, especially the final battle, they are remembered as winners. Rose was a winner, even though she lost the biggest battle of her life. It was a battle that was the final pages of her life, but not the final words. Rose is a hero who was in our midst, and her memory still is.

> \* *According to the American Cancer Society, any of the following unusual changes in the breast can be a symptom of breast cancer: swelling of all or part of the breast, skin irritation or dimpling, breast pain, nipple pain or the nipple turning inward, redness, scaliness, or thickening of the nipple or breast skin, a nipple discharge other than breast milk, or a lump in the underarm area.*

> \*\**According to Breast Cancer.org, in 2011, an estimated 230,480 new cases of invasive breast cancer were expected to be diagnosed in women in the U.S., and about 2,140 new cases of invasive breast cancer were expected to be diagnosed in men in 2011. A man's lifetime risk of breast cancer is about 1 in 1,000.*

***According* to Breast Cancer Awareness, about 39,520
women in the U.S. were expected to die in 2011 from
breast cancer, though death rates have been decreasing
since 1990 — especially in women under age 50.*

# THOSE LEFT BEHIND

THE FOOTSTEPS OF Rose's life left an impression in her community and especially within her family; an impression that would stick for a long time. The last two weeks in Rose's life flew by too fast for Thomas, Olivia, and Abigail. All three of them were in a fog through the funeral. The perfume of Rose's life was everywhere, and the notes from the music that she played on her beloved grand piano lingered, even two weeks after the last time she played. Her paintings on the walls share her talent with everyone who enters the house, in other homes, and even on the walls of the municipal buildings in the town and county. The flowers that she had planted in her yard would bloom as a memorial to her for years to come.

The first few weeks after Rose passed away, Thomas was busy with legal issues and bill paying from her illness and death. He tried to be so busy that he couldn't think of anything but what he was doing, because when he did, he would think of her; no matter how hard he tried to keep thoughts of his beloved wife, from mind and heart. Sleeping was hard for him because the echo of her voice was everywhere. He missed her so much, and had never known such pain. Just as it was hard for him to go to sleep, he did not want to wake up, because when he slept he dreamt of Rose. Why would he ever want to wake up from being with his Rose? No matter how hard he tried to keep dreaming, he always woke up alone.

Thomas always knew that grieving was a process, but he felt grief in waves. Sometimes his grief was so deep that he could hardly move. Sometimes his heart and mind was so clouded by it that it was difficult for him to make decisions, even simple ones. He had never realized how much he'd relied on Rose to help with his businesses and taking care of the home, until she was gone. As he struggled with these chores, the waves of his grief grew even deeper.

He and his wife shared so many interests that when he tried to do any of them by himself, his grief was enough to get him to stop in the middle of the activity. His friends kindly checked in with him at least for a little while. Always, the focus was on how he was doing without Rose. After a while, even his friends stopped checking on him. It wasn't that they had stopped caring; it was just that others grieving make so many people uncomfortable. His friends still came by, but they stopped talking about Rose for the most part, so Thomas was alone with his grief.

After about six months some of his friends, especially the ladies, began to suggest ladies for him to do things with. He appreciated his friends' kindness though he really wasn't ready to date. He took a few of these ladies to some events, but he always found himself silently comparing them to Rose and they just didn't measure up. He finally decided it just wasn't time to socialize one on one just yet. He would limit his socializing to big group activities for a little while longer.

Olivia stayed at her parents' home for two weeks after her mother died to help her father and sister with things before she went back to her home in Virginia. She gathered as many mementos as she could of her mother that she would lovingly display at her home. She and her sister shared their grief together those weeks by frequently crying together. Their tears helped make their grief a little easier for them both. The sisters have always been close, but their mother's death brought them closer. The last day with her father and sister was the hardest day for her, since her mother's passing was for her. She didn't want to leave and had delayed her leaving two times, but if she wanted to keep her job, she had to be back at work the next day. Sadly and reluctantly, she bid farewell to her father and sister, with the promise that she would call them every day.

Abigail had been especially close to her mother, close enough to choose a college near home to go to and close enough to find a job nearby. About the time her mother got sick, she found an apartment that she really liked and was fixing to move into it, but canceled plans when her mother became sick. Seeing her mother waste away and in so much pain was hard enough, but it was even harder after she was gone. How she longed to hear her mother say, "I love you." How she wished she could feel her hug, just one more time. She always turned to her mother when she was upset or needed advice. Her sister was always there for her, but there were certain things that Abigail did not want Olivia to know about her life. She was lost without her mother, even to share her grief with, though she knew that was a silly thought but her mother would understand.

Abigail had a job that she loved, but when her mother became very ill, she arranged to work part time for a little while until things settled down. There was so much her mother did to keep the home running smoothly. After a couple of weeks of trying to do what her mother had done for so many years, Abigail said in exasperation, " I had no idea of how many things my mother did just to keep our home running. You couldn't pay me enough to do everything she did around the home. To think that she didn't do it for money, she did it for us."

One of the favorite things that Rose enjoyed doing was cooking, especially southern style. She never objected when anyone helped her cook; she actually loved having help. She particularly enjoyed having her daughters cook with her, but didn't insist on it. Her daughters knew the basics of cooking, but not like their mother. After Rose died, Abigail took it upon herself to cook the family meals. There were some rocky meals in the beginning, but after a spell, her cooking improved a lot; but to Abigail, she had a long ways to go to be as good as her mother. She felt her mother with her in the kitchen, so she found herself in the kitchen more. The more she cooked, the more she enjoyed it.

Other activities that Rose did for the joy of doing them took much more time and creativity than Thomas or Abigail had been aware of. Even tending the flower gardens that Rose loved so much wasn't as easy as she had made it look. This was a task that Thomas took on thinking that wouldn't be terribly difficult, since he ran a landscaping business. He found out that her gardens required painstaking detail that he wasn't aware of. He was glad he had taken on her flower gardens, because as he worked on them, he felt her with him.

After a while, new memories were created for Thomas, Olivia, and Abigail. Daily living routines that Rose was no longer involved in took over a great deal of daily focus for them all. Their grief ached in their hearts, because their loss never went away; it just wasn't as obvious to those around them. In summer night skies, when a full moon came up and the sky sparkled with stars, each of them would look up and feel her absence deeply, and long for just one more touch from a lady who meant the world to them.

Grief is a natural reaction to loss. Losing someone we love to cancer is just one of the many causes of grief. Those who bravely fight cancer are heroes, but so are the ones who support, stand by, and are left behind by the cancer fighters who lose. The feeling of their loss is described as grief. At first, it's the prime focus. Grief is actually a process. The grieving process includes Shock and Denial, Intense Concern, Despair and Depression, and Recovery. After a while, grief evolves from being a prime focus to being among the focuses in the lives of those suffering the loss of a loved one.

There are about eight million cancer deaths per year worldwide. There are at least twenty-four million new heroes every year because of cancer's awful toll. These heroes are in all walks of life, doing their best to carry on in spite of their great loss. We do business and we shop with them. We work with them and socialize with them. They are wearing suits and dresses, they are wearing shorts and tee shirts, and sometimes, they are heroes in blue jeans. We are in the midst of heroes, we just have to look for them.

# HEROES WHO HELP

# BECAUSE HE'S NEEDED

CARL GOES TO bed when the rest of the world is going to work. He works from seven in the evening to seven in the morning. He is supposed to work just four days but because of heavy medical bills from when his wife was ill six years ago and large student loans he works five and sometimes six days per week. For some reason he is tired a lot.

When Carl leaves work it takes him ten minutes to get home. After he enters the door of his home Carl hugs, kisses and greets his wife, son, and daughter. He bends down to pet the cat for a few seconds or so. He then grabs a quick snack, watches the news for a little while, gets on the computer to read and respond to his email. About an hour later if he can stay awake that long he heads to bed. Sometimes Carl takes ten minutes give or take a few minutes to prepare for bed, other times he falls asleep before he gets that far.

Carl usually sleeps for four hours but sometimes he is so tired that he might sleep for five hours. He awakens between one and two o'clock in the afternoon. By the time he shaves, cleans up, allows himself to have some quiet time and gets dressed it is about three. He moves to the kitchen making a sandwich or microwaves to eat. After he finishes eating for two hours he takes care of household chores, phone calls he needs to make and whatever else is on the to do list his wife left him before she went to work in the morning.

Carl's wife arrives home at about three thirty. His children if they are not involved in after school activities and they usually are arrive home at three forty five. When his children are involved in after school activities Carl will not see his children awake except when he sees them briefly in the morning before they go to school. Carl's son is the starting full back on his high school football team. He is a senior and has been a letterman since he was a sophomore. Carl is lucky if he sees him in two games per year. His daughter is a talented violinist. She has been in an orchestra since she was six. Since she entered middle school she has been in a band and a community orchestra. All of her concerts are at night usually at seven or seven thirty which is when Carl begins work. He can count on one hand the concerts that she has performed at that he was able to attend. Once in while he was able to attend the first part of some of her concerts but when he did get to the first part of her concerts she didn't always perform in the beginning.

To make up for his time away from his family during the school year his hospital allows him to take vacations a week at Christmas and extended vacations in the summer so that he can spend quality time with his family. It still is hard not to be able to see his son play football very often or miss as many of his daughter's concerts as he does, but he does get to hear her play when she performs at summer concerts so knowing that he will get to hear her play in the summer makes it easier. Unfortunately there just aren't any summer football games except when he and his son organize a touch football game for his guy friends and family. The losing team always buys the winning team pizza. Since Carl's son has been on his team he hasn't had to buy pizza.

Carl's wife is Carl's best friend and is always supportive. She is a great mother, an even better wife and keeps things running smoothly at home. Six years ago he thought his wife was going to die. She had stage three breast cancer but she became one of the lucky survivors of breast cancer. There were so many people who helped her in the hospital but she was especially thankful for the nurses who eased her pain and fear. Carl is a nurse, not one of her nurses except at home but a nurse none the less.

Carl is not just any nurse. He works the night shift at County Hospital. Of the two hospitals in the city County

Hospital is the only one that takes people who can't pay for hospital care. The care that is given at County is the same good care for every patient regardless of their ability to pay. At County Hospital every patient is important. Carl's job is not as exciting as working in an emergency room or as emotionally touching as working in a Delivery Room or a maternity ward but his job is just as important. He takes care of patients in the intensive care unit. His job is to help very sick or very injured patients improve their health enough to be moved out of the intensive care unit or ICU to private or semi-private rooms in the hospital.

Sometimes his patients get sicker in spite of his efforts and sometimes they even die. He doesn't see any visitors except for family members because of how gravely ill or hurt his patients are and because of the hours he works. Those who he does see are worried and upset. A part of his job is to help patients' families as well as to care for his patients. Many of his patients have not had anyone who actually was interested in helping them when they weren't so sick care in such a very time. Carl's kindness to every patient is known throughout the hospital and even outside of the hospital.

Carl has been offered quite a few jobs in other hospitals. Some were quite attractive offers but none have been even tempting except for the offer from the hospital where his wife was in and for considerably more money than he is making at County Hospital. This offer was really tempting. He talked it over with his wife but they both agreed that he gets a lot of satisfaction from helping and caring for people who are not used to kindness of any kind at County Hospital. The patients at the other hospital would still benefit from his care but they are not the same kind of people who usually go to County Hospital. Carl would not have the same sort of impact on them as he does at County Hospital. The other hospital would be an exciting place to work in Carl thought but he would never be needed more than he is needed at County Hospital. The money was hard to turn down though.

When Carl was first hired by County Hospital he

worked days in the recovery room. He enjoyed being the first person that patients saw when they woke up after surgery. He enjoyed the fact that he was able to help people who were hurting feel better. For the first few years working in the recovery room at County Hospital was an incredible experience. His days were filled to overflowing, his young family and beautiful wife at home made him happier than he ever remembered being.

After a few years he began to think how nice it would be to be able to work with patients for more than just a few hours. He began to look at possibly working at another department in the hospital. For a long time he couldn't find another department that he liked better than the recovery room. About the time he began his fourth year at County he noticed that there always seemed to be openings in ICU on the night shift. There were a lot fewer in openings on the day shift in every department. He began to be more and more curious about the possibility of working the ICU on the night shift. As Carl looked in to what the night shift had to offer he found out that those who worked nights were paid more than those who work days. There was also more opportunity for working overtime. This was especially interesting to Carl as his medical bills and student loan payments were difficult to manage on the salary from his job as a recovery room nurse. His student loans would have been manageable on his salary from working days if the bills for his wife's cancer weren't so overwhelming. As it became harder and harder to stretch his paycheck even with his wife's new job, his thoughts kept going towards working the night shift.

Carl had a friend who was the night supervisor in the intensive care unit at the hospital who had wanted him to work for him as soon as he had met Carl. One day Carl arrived at work early to find out more about the IC at night. His friend offered him the charge nurse position. When Carl told him he wasn't qualified for being a charge nurse, his friend told him that he had already signed him up for the necessary training. He explained what Carl already knew that the intensive care unit night shift had a hard time keeping people. He went on to say that what the ICU night shift needed was a really good charge nurse, someone like Carl who by their leadership could bring stability to the shift which would keep people from quitting. He told Carl that he was confident that he would be a great fit for night shift. He found himself considering it but still he wasn't sure that he wanted to give up normal hours.

Not long after his visit Carl's friend called him on his day off and asked him to return a cell phone he accidently on purpose left in Car's car the day before. Carl didn't remember his friend leaving his cell phone in his car but when he went to look for it sure enough he found it in his glove compartment. When Carl went to the ICU to give his friend his phone back he was invited to meet the staff and really showed him around. His friend introduced him as the new charge nurse even though Carl had not agreed to be the charge nurse yet.

There was something about the ICU night shift that drew Carl. He knew that if he could just keep the people he had just met and encourage a few other good people to work with them patient care in the ICU at night would be as good as or better than the day shift. As Carl's friend figured he would Carl gave notice right after he left the ICU. Before he actually started working the ICU he took the necessary training to be charge nurse and began working the night shift soon after.

Carl is if not the best charge nurse ever at County Hospital just one of the best. There are no longer many openings on the ICU night shift any more. There is in fact a list of nurses, patient care technicians and more who want to work night shift on his floor. Patient care at the ICU at night has never been better. The hospital has a large file of thank you notes from patients and their families who have been cared for by Carl and his staff at County Hospital. Carl continues to look for ways to improve patient care and the way he looks out after those who work with him. Carl's successes continue to make his friend Carl's friend look good, real good for hiring him.

Anyone who has ever worked the hours that Carl and

his staff do know that that working those hours has it's down side. Staying awake during the early hours can be very difficult and being wide awake while caring for patients is critical. It can be easy to miss important changes in patients' condition even when wide awake. When things are busy staying awake is not hard but when the floor becomes quiet staying awake becomes critical. Exhaustion is a real issue for nurses and hospital staff who work the night shift. It is a problem that Carl deals with. Carl is not alone with this challenge. Nurses drink more coffee than any other profession.

Three months after Carl began working the ICU at night he thought that as much as enjoyed working his new job he might have to go back to working days as he was not able to spend enough time with his family. He asked for a meeting with his friend. His friend understood Carl's concern and was afraid he would lose him so he offered to give Carl a week off at Christmas, extended time off during the summer and days off for birthdays and his anniversary. He also increased his pay. Carl stayed.

Carl enjoys his job as much as anyone can. He plans on working night shift for a very long time. The only change will be that he will work less overtime as he gets older. He tells his friends and relatives he doesn't like to be a nurse he needs to be a nurse. Reaching out to help people is the very heart of who he is.

It is not hard to think of nurses as heroes at least the nurses that everyone sees during visiting hours. Nurses as well as other members of hospital staffs everywhere go to great lengths to save lives and to help those whose lives are saved live better. No day time nurse would ever admit to being a hero and no one else who works alongside them would admit to being hero either. When lives are threatened heroes run in to help. Anyone who has ever witnessed nurses and the ones who work with them have seen them running to help people just like heroes do. Those who work after hours in hospitals, the ones few people see are heroes too. They reach out to others putting the lives of their patients ahead of their own even giving up rest to make sure that their patients and the their patients' families feel rest. They don't worry about being heroes or not being heroes. They only worry about providing quality patient care. We are in the midst of heroes even the ones we don't see.

# A FAMILY THAT LOVES ME

KATHLEEN WAS A beautiful child. When she was born and for the first forty-two months of her life her daddy and mommy thought that Kathleen was a perfect child, a real princess. Her daddy was a respected minister and community leader. Her mama was a stay at homemaker who also came from a much respected family. To the community they were the perfect young family. For awhile they were. Kathleen was extremely well behaved until she reached the age of three and a half.

When she reached three and a half she began to misbehave like a typical toddler. In public her daddy laughed it off but behind closed doors he beat her with whatever he could get his hands on, a belt, a stick of wood a pan or even a broom stick. She didn't even have to misbehave. Her daddy had to just think she was giving a look that she was about to misbehave and he would beat her.

Her mommy couldn't help Kathleen as she was an alcoholic and was drunk most of the time. She had fewer and fewer days of sobriety. At first her mama in her drunken stupor would try to stop her daddy from hurting Kathleen but he would beat her too. After awhile her mama stopped trying to help her. Her focus became more and more on the bottle.

Kathleen's abuse was to go on for four years. He daddy told her that she was to blame for her abuse. That if she was a better little girl he wouldn't have to correct her so hard. In all of those years he continued to give great sermons or so his congregation said. By the time Kathleen was six everyone in town knew that her mommy was an alcoholic and drunk most of the time so their sympathies went to the minister who was trying to raise his daughter without the help of her mommy.

Kathleen's abuse became more and more obvious so her daddy stopped sending her to school. So that she could go to church he had Kathleen's mommy apply makeup to cover up her bruises. Kathleen was terrified of her daddy but if she even looked a little afraid or let one tear fall he would beat her even worse than at other times. In spite of her abuse Kathleen still was a beautiful little girl and still wanted to please adults. She was smart and wanted to so badly go to school. Her daddy knew that if she did go to school his abuse would quickly be noticed and so he told everyone he was homeschooling her but he did very little homeschooling. The best that he did was to teach her to read the Bible. She was given no other book to read.

Jean was a nurse who worked for an adoption agency. She was more of a social worker/ nurse. She loved working to match adoptive parents with the right children. She selflessly did this job for fifteen years. Her boss confided in her about the shortage of good foster parents and hinted that she should become a foster parent. She told Jean that there was such a need for foster parents. Jean told her that she enjoyed the work that she did but wasn't sure she wanted to take her work home at night. Being a foster parent for Jean would be just like taking her work home.

Her boss kept hinting at Jean becoming a foster parent. Jean kept telling her no but her boss didn't give up. Finally her boss got to a point to where she asked Jean to take all of the foster parent classes, have all of the background checking done, have her home inspected and finger prints done so that if she ever changed her mind and was ready to have a foster child that they could take care of things right away. Jean agreed to do it if for no other reason than it would get her boss to stop pestering her about being a foster parent. It did for awhile.

Soon after Jean and her husband had done everything necessary to be foster parents her boss started up trying to get her to take a child. Jean's response was that for her to take foster child she would have to be somebody very special. Her boss told her that she saw several 'somebodys special' every week.

Kathleen's life got worse and worse. Her daddy's congregation became concerned over Kathleen's well-being because of how bad her mommy disease had grown. Her daddy tried to keep her from being drunk in public for a long time but as her disease progressed even he couldn't keep her alcoholism hidden. Kathleen's mommy condition embarrassed her daddy. When he was embarrassed he took it out on Kathleen hurting her more than ever.

Kathleen was a child hurting without anyone to offer her the help that she so badly needed. Several of the church ladies grew concerned about Kathleen and paid a visit to their preacher's family. Before they got to the front door they heard what seemed to be loud crying and someone saying 'I'm sorry' over and over again. The Deacon's wife knocked on the door no one answered. She knocked again still no answer. She tried the door and it opened.

The church women walked in to the house and in the direction of the crying. They found Kathleen's mother beaten and bloody crying and saying 'I'm sorry'. They were certain that Kathleen's mother had beaten her until they got a closer look at Kathleen's mother and then surmised that she was apologizing to Kathleen for not protecting her better. At first they didn't see Kathleen as she was barely standing in the shadows of the room bruised and bloodied like her mommy. She wasn't crying. She wasn't making a sound. Her eyes were wide with terror.

Kathleen's mother told them that she did something she hadn't done in a very long time. Her husband was beating Kathleen as he did so often. This time she stood up to her husband and tried to protect her only child. For a brief moment her motherly instincts were stronger than the disease of alcoholism. For her courage he turned on her and beat her almost as badly as he beat Kathleen.

What the church women discovered was not what they expected to find. Before going in to the preacher's house they were sure that they would find an abused child not an abused woman and child. They had an idea recently that Kathleen was being hurt but not her mommy. They thought that she was the one who was hurting Kathleen.

After seeing the condition of Kathleen and her mother they realized that they were very wrong that day. The Deacon's wife cleaned Kathleen and her mommy up and tried to get them to leave the preacher but Kathleen's mommy wouldn't and it was hard to get Kathleen out of the shadows.. Kathleen wouldn't or couldn't speak. They weren't sure. Her long hair was matted and she was very thin. Her eyes had a wide eyed look of terror that never left her. The ladies tried to take Kathleen away but she ran from them.

The Deacon's wife quickly ran across the street and asked to use their telephone. She called a nurse friend and social worker to come check out both Kathleen and her mommy. The nurse was Jean's niece. She examined Kathleen and her mommy. Kathleen had many scars from previous beating along with broken bones that had healed but had never been set. Her mommy didn't have as many scars and broken bones as Kathleen had but it was obvious that she had been beaten often. With help Kathleen and her mommy were put in ambulances and sent to the hospital for more thorough evaluations.

Kathleen was very quickly identified as an abused child. Another social worker was called to find a placement for her in a foster home. Her mommy was abused but also was an alcoholic with major liver damage even at her young age so it was harder to find help for her than it was for Kathleen. As soon as Kathleen's daddy found out where his daughter and wife were he stormed the hospital where he was met by the church board and the city Police Chief. He was told he no long was the preacher for his church and the Police Chief told him that he was not to go in to the hospital. He told him that they were preparing to arrest him even though there were no laws to protect women and children from abuse but they would find other charges to arrest him for.

Kathleen's daddy made a feeble attempt to demand that they give him back his wife and daughter. He left town a month later and was not seen or heard from again. Kathleen's mommy was placed in a program to help her with her alcoholism but she was never able to stay sober for very long and never got her daughter back though every five years or so she would visit her.

As soon as Social Services got a call to help Kathleen, Jean's boss called her and said, "You know how you have said that for you to take a foster child they would have to be special?"

Jean said, "Yes I did." Her boss said, "We have a little girl who is very special. Her name is Kathleen. We believe that she is very bright but can't tell for sure since we have not been able to get her to communicate at all. We don't believe that she has felt love in a very long time. We are not sure if she can't talk or won't talk. She needs someone who can love her like she hasn't been loved in a very long time. We think you are just the folks who can do it. We will do something that we never do for any of the other foster parents. We will let you meet Kathleen and then you can decide if you to be her foster parents."

Jean told her boss that she wouldn't make any promises but would meet the little girl at the social services building. Jean called her husband to meet her there. They met in the parking lot and entered in to the building. When they saw her she was standing forlornly as far away from the social worker and Jean's boss as she could stand. Her eyes were large making it obvious that she was afraid. They both fell in love with her as soon as they saw her. When they tried to get closer to her she moved away from them. When they talked to her she looked in their direction and trembled. Jean was certain that Kathleen's hearing was good but her fear made her mute.

Jean and her husband asked her boss and the social worker if they could be Kathleen's foster parents. Her boss said she would be upset if they weren't. They then asked Kathleen if she wanted to come home with them. She took two steps closer to them and nodded her head slightly.

Jean's family was large, loving and happy. There was always a full house. Jean had taken this for granted until the day she brought Kathleen home. Jean knew that Kathleen needed to feel love. She wanted to hold her in her arms and love away all of the hurt, all of the pain and all of the fear that Kathleen had experienced in her short life. She knew at least for now that the worst thing she could was to reach out to her.

Jean was going to have Kathleen begin her life in her new family by having her start out sleeping in the guest room and then finding the best of her daughters to pair her up with. Her oldest daughter had other ideas. As soon as they entered the house her daughter greeted Kathleen and said, "Hi my name is Ellen. I'm your new sister. You and I get to share a bedroom. I hope you like it. She took Kathleen by the hand and brought her to her new room. This was a room that her daughter had fought hard for, her own private room. Ellen was a teenager and felt like she needed a room to herself. Jean agreed. Ellen hadn't had her own room for very long. Jean could hardly believe that after Ellen fought so hard for her room she was so willing to share it with Kathleen. There already seemed to be a bond between the two of them.

Ellen let Kathleen get used to the room and came out to talk to her mother. She told her mother that before her parents brought Kathleen home she never thought that she would be willing to give up her privacy but as soon as she saw Kathleen there was such a deep sadness and loneliness in her eyes that she just melted. "I couldn't even think of her in any room but mine. Is that OK?" Jean felt her eyes tearing up as she reached out to hug Ellen.

Kathleen didn't stay in her room long. She came out near where Ellen was but not too close. Her eyes now took on warmth and a look of wonder. Jean was afraid that that with so many people coming and going in her home it would be too much for Kathleen. That day there were more visitors than usual because word got out about the new family member. Though Kathleen didn't speak the love and good wishes from all who came to the house seemed to feed her loved starved heart. By the time she went to bed she was so near to Ellen she could have been her shadow.

For the first few weeks that Kathleen was part of Jean's family it was like water to a dry plant but she still showed fear. Jean wasn't sure what she was afraid of exactly but she knew she was afraid. Arguing and shouting in anyway upset Kathleen though she never cried. She grew closer to Jean, Jeans husband and Ellen every day but had also begun to follow her other new sisters and brothers around.

About the fourth week Jean asked Kathleen to help set the table. As she was carrying some plates she tripped and dropped the plates breaking most of them. She ran to the darkest part of the room, covering her head with arms with her eyes tightly closed and moaned. Jean came over to her took her in arms rocking her back and forth saying, "That's OK baby that's OK" over and over again until Kathleen stopped moaning and opened her eyes.

When she opened her eyes she scanned Jean's face, her eyes going up and down and back and forth. Jean still hugging her said, "I love you." Ellen standing nearby said, "You are family. We all love you honey." Kathleen's eyes for the first time in a very long time filled with tears. Also for the first time in a very long time Kathleen cleared her throat a couple of times and said, "I love you mommy." She hugged Jean back so tightly Jean could hardly breathe and then suddenly ran to Ellen with her arms outstretched and hugged Ellen saying, "I love you sis." From that moment on it seemed as though Kathleen had so much to say that she could hardly stop talking even for bed. One night soon after Kathleen had begun to talk, Jean was walking past Ellen and Kathleen's room and she heard Ellen say, "It is time to stop talking now Kathleen so that you can rest your talker for tomorrow." A few minutes later Jean heard Ellen's weary but patient voice firmly say, "Honey no more talking. We both need to rest." Jean walked quietly by their room.

A few days later Jean awoke at 5:00 AM to the sound of a vacuum cleaner. For a few minutes Jean couldn't figure out what the sound was. When she identified it as a vacuum cleaner she still didn't understand why it was running. She ran to where the sound of the vacuum cleaner was running and saw Kathleen finishing up vacuuming the living room rug. As Jean looked in astonishment she noticed that all of the dusting was done not just in the living room but in the kitchen and family room too. Not only that but all of dishes were put away in the kitchen, the floor was swept and washed and there was a load of washing in the washing machine and another in the dryer. She also had the ironing board set up to iron clothes as soon as they were done in the dryer.

Jean hugged Kathleen and thanked her for all that she had done. She asked her why she had been up so early working so hard. Kathleen said, "Oh mommy I am so sorry I should have been doing this as soon as I became your little girl. My old daddy would beat me if I didn't have all of this done when he came home and when my mommy took her medicine I tried so hard to help her make dinner for daddy. He always got mad at me. Last night I remembered that I hadn't done any of those things for you. I am so sorry."

Kathleen looked up at Jean who in spite of trying not to cry was crying anyway after hearing what little Kathleen. She misunderstood Jean's tears and said, "Mommy I'm sorry. I promise I won't forget to do my chores ever again."

Jean hugged her again and said, "Honey around here everyone helps. We all work together. No one is expected to do as much as you did this morning. I have some chores just for you that I expect you to do but they are not hard, not like you did this morning. You did too much work and you will never have to work as hard as you did at your old house again. You will not iron those clothes in the washer and dryer. I have a few other children who need to learn how to iron and they will take over from you but not for another two hours. Now go to bed and be careful that you don't wake Ellen."

Jean enrolled Kathleen in school. Though Kathleen started school a little later than most children she was a smart little girl and hard worker. It wasn't long before she was allowed to skip a grade and then a little while later she was able to skip another grade. She finished high school third in her class. Jean wanted to adopt her but in hopes that one day Kathleen's mother might be able to finally overcome her alcoholism Kathleen stayed as a Jean's foster daughter but to the family Kathleen was a daughter, sister and later on a well-loved auntie.

Her foster mother inspired Kathleen to become a nurse. When she fell in love and was married it was her foster daddy who gave her away. She is now a great auntie and grandmother well-loved in a larger than ever, more loving than ever family, always feeling gratitude to having a mother who loved her, a sister who became her best friend and sisters and brothers who taught her what true love meant.

Heroes are people who give of themselves. There cannot be people who give more of themselves than do foster parents. We are in the midst of heroes taking care of about four hundred thousand foster children every day in the United States.

*On average, foster parents in the Unites States receive about $500 per month or $6000 per year to take care of each foster child. In 2009 The US Department of Agriculture estimated it to cost between $11,650 and $13,530 annually to raise a child. According to Wikipedia there are about four hundred thousand children receiving foster care in 2009 down from over 500,000 in 2000.*

# THE CAREGIVER

DARLEEN IS A caregiver for Lenny, who has dementia. Since there are at least ten different types of dementia, Darleen is not sure what type he has. For Darleen, all that matters is that she makes life as good for him as she can, even as he slowly loses what makes him Lenny. She works with him as he loses more and more of his memory and personality. As she sees it, Lenny is falling down a dark hole and there is nothing he can do about it; her job is to ease the fall.

Darleen is a patient care technician. She began her career working in a nursing home, where she worked with many patients who were going through the various stages of dementia. She was troubled by the fact that as much as she and her co-workers cared for their patients, their work load was so high and they were spread so thin, the best that they could do was to take care of their patients basic needs.

Darleen knew that nursing home care was expensive for the families. She also knew that many patients gave their life savings, sold their homes and gave the money made on the sale of their homes, and even their children's inheritance to the owners of the nursing home while they were patients at the homes, as payment for their care. Darleen felt it was terrible that dementia victims couldn't stay at their own home where there were some things that would be familiar to them, or at the very least ghosts of things that were familiar to them. She frequently thought it'd be less expensive for the families to have a full time caregiver than to put them in a nursing home.

She felt bad how few patients have visitors on a regular basis. She heard from those who visited infrequently that when they came to the nursing home for a visit, the patient they came to visit didn't even remember them at all, so they didn't see the point in visiting any more often. In spite of what these people said, Darleen knew better, she knew how much visits meant to her patients even if they didn't know who was visiting them or after they left if they had visited with them at all. She knew that these visits represented kindness, even love, which still bridged the chasm of the encroaching darkness of dementia. Darlene felt like even if the memories of those who visited were gone from her patients, visiting them was the right thing to do. It seemed to Darlene that not many felt the way she did. After about three years of working at the nursing home, Darleen grew disillusioned and discouraged, feeling overworked and worn out. In spite of the fact that Darleen loved her patients dearly, she was forced to quit working at the nursing home.

When Darleen began to work at the nursing home, her aunt was showing signs of early dementia. By the time Darleen quit her job, her cousins had reached a point where they needed to either put their mother in a nursing home, or find someone to care for her. Within days of leaving the nursing home, Darleen's cousins offered her the job of caring for their mother. They knew what a caring woman Darleen was and knew how much she loved her aunt. Darleen accepted the offer gladly and began her new career, a career that she was that she was going to give her all to, and one that she was to be very good at.

Soon after Darleen began to care for her aunt, she joined a support group for family members and caregivers for victims of dementia. When Darleen wasn't looking after her aunt, she researched the latest and best practices for dementia care, and she would put into practice what she learned as she cared for her aunt. Among the many things that she learned, she found out that there were certain colors that made it harder for people who have dementia. She made sure that she neither wore those colors, nor had them in her aunt's home.

Darleen had always loved her aunt, but the more time she spent with her, the more her heart went out to her.

She felt her aunt's anger at her illness, her feelings of total helplessness, confusion, fears, and hopelessness as her aunt felt the blackness of dementia reaching out and overtaking her. Darleen wished that she had a magic pill, magic wand, or anything to help her. She didn't realize that she was giving her aunt the only thing that she could give her that would mean anything, that would stay with her even if she would only be able to remember the feelings she had. Darleen gave her aunt love, kindness, warmth, and caring.

After four years and three months of care, Darlene's aunt's body ended its journey when she succumbed to the flu. Her uncle and cousins would always be grateful to Darlene for the care she gave to her aunt those four years and three months of her life. Her cousins felt like Darlene's love and kindness allowed her to slow the loss of their mother, or at the very least keep the best part of her alive as long as was possible, her loving nature.

Three weeks after Darleen's aunt died, one of the local leaders of the dementia support group called her and asked if she would be able to become a caregiver for a sixty year old woman named Cathy. Cathy's dementia had progressed fairly quickly and she'd already lost a great deal of her memory. Darleen became Cathy's full time caregiver for five years and seven months, until she died of a massive heart attack. Cathy's family felt the same way about Darleen that her cousins and uncle felt about her. They were very grateful to Darleen for treating Cathy with dignity at the same time dementia was robbing her of her natural dignity.

After Cathy died, Darleen thought she might take a break from caring for people with dementia, and for a little, while she did. Her break lasted for seven weeks, because she missed what she loved doing best. About the same time, a neighbor a block away had reached the point where he could no longer live by himself. He had dementia, and had been having some memory loss for the last eight years, but now he couldn't live by himself any longer. In the last ten days, he started five small fires and would forget where the three bathrooms were in his house. Sending him to a nursing home was out of the question. His daughter knew Darleen from when they were children. Lenny's daughter lived a five hour flight from where she grew up, and had just arrived at her childhood home just three hours earlier to find a caregiver for her dad. She had decided to take a walk to clear her head before she began her search. Darleen was planting some flowers in her front yard when Lenny's daughter saw her. She couldn't believe it was Darleen, since it had been so many years since they had last seen each other. To be on the safe side she called out her name. Darleen looked up, saw her old friend, wiped her hands and ran to her; she was so excited to see her. They hugged and began to catch up on their busy lives. When Darleen discussed her career, Lenny's daughter jumped in and said, "Darleen, daddy needs your help. Please say you'll care for him" and so Darleen began to make life easier for yet another person.

Heroes come in all shapes and sizes. Some heroes are very big, while some are very small. Heroes are said to be people who do something noble. There can be no activity more noble than saving someone's dignity. The Alzheimer's Association estimates that 5.2 million Americans age 65 and older are living with Alzheimer's. This means that there are at least 5.2 million caregivers/heroes. We are in the midst of heroes, we just have to look for them.

# SAVING THE FARM

PHIL IS RACING the clock. He worked long on his first job than he should have so is running late to get ready for his second job. His wife already has his lunch and a big thermos of coffee ready for him. He wishes that he didn't have to take time for a shower but he is covered with dirt, dust and grime. He has no choice but to take a shower. As he showers he finds out that even his hair has dirt in it so washing his hair has to be done as well. He is not sorry that he is running late as he got a lot done outside. He moves as quickly as he can through his shower. He shaves rather haphazardly but gets most of his beard.

After the shower he barely takes time to dry himself off. He quickly puts on his uniform and getting ready to go to a job he didn't like after spending a day doing what he loved. He looks at his watch and it is almost ten fifteen. He has only ten minutes to go before he has to leave the house. He normally doesn't work as late outside as he did tonight but it had rained a lot this spring which made it too wet to do what he did today earlier and the window for doing it was quickly coming closing.

Phil visits the rooms of his fourteen year old son Paul, twelve year old daughter Shari and ten year old Tina who he calls Tiny. Paul is awake. Paul asked Phil how it went today. Phil told him that he got everything finished and just in time too, it started to rain by the time he got to the end of the last row. In the few minutes it took to get off of the tractor and to the house the sky opened up and it is still raining hard. Both of his daughters were asleep. Before he kissed each one of them on their foreheads, he thought how beautiful his girls were he told both of them to have sweet dreams. Tina mumbled, "Night daddy and burrowed deep in her pillow deep in her dreams.

He races to the kitchen, kisses his wife Pam good by grabs his lunch and an extra sandwich and a carbonated water. Before he leaves the house he tells his wife how much he loves her and how sorry he is that he has to work nights but that his job at night will allow take away a lot of the worries of losing their farm.

Phil works as a security guard for a warehouse at from 11PM to 7 AM. He looks more important than he is. He carries a radio and a gun but does not expect to ever use the gun. He could use it if he has to. He has been a good shot since he was eight. His daddy used to take him hunting with him almost as soon as he could walk. He is a good enough shot to always bag his limit of deer and wild pig. He does use his radio for radio checks twice each shift and has used it once in a while when he has seen something suspicious in and around the warehouse.

Being a security guard is not a hard a job. He has to do rounds checking on every work area and every office twice an hour. He has to do a perimeter and parking lot walk twice each shift. Before the end of each shift he has a short form he has to fill out which is not hard. If he notices anything suspicious after he checks it out and calls it in he has to fill out a longer form. He has a fair amount of free time on his hands so Phil has enrolled in an online college master's degree program for business administration. His hope is that having this degree will allow him a chance to work part time for a farm supply company in management position that will open up in a year or so. This will allow him more time to work on the farm. He knows about the position because one of their representatives approached him with the possibility of hiring him when he earns his master's degree. If he gets the job his wife can work part time too.

If being a security guard was Phil's only job he would hate it but it's not. It's a job Phil took to save the career he really loves, that career is farming. He has a small farm of two hundred and fifty acres. He is a fourth generation farmer. He is the fourth member of his family to have inherited the farm. He hopes his children will be the next generation. This is a farm that was passed down to him by his daddy. His grandfather passed the farm though it was a larger farm to his daddy and his grandfather inherited the farm from Phil's great grandfather.

Phil farms mostly corn but he farms peanuts as well and is considering building some chicken barns. The farm he grew up on was considerably larger than the one he has now but when the farm was going through some lean years to keep the farm going his daddy had to sell some of farm to keep most of it. Phil has had to do the same with some more of the farm. It hurts him every time h thinks of it. He hopes one day to buy the land back but isn't sure when he will be able to afford to. He has reached a point where the only way he will sell any more land is if he will be forced to sell the whole farm. If he ever reaches that point it will kill him. Every time he takes a step outside of the house he thinks about how grand it will be to pass the farm down to his children but for the farm to be worth passing down it has to be large enough farm to pass down to his children when they get old enough.

About three years ago his wife went back to work as a dental hygienist. She is a farm girl who loves everything about the family farm. She wasn't always a farm girl. She was raised in a big city. Her daddy is a dentist. When she fell in love with Phil she fell in love with farming. Before they were married she worked as a dental hygienist briefly. After they were married she became a farmer's wife and farms right along with Phil. She loves being a farmer's wife. Going back to work as a hygienist is part of farming it's helping to save the farm. She thinks that if the farm had been damaged or destroyed by a hurricane, tornado or fire she would be working hard to save even rebuild the farm. By cleaning teeth she in fact is working hard to save and even one day restore the farm by buying back the land that they were forced to sell. She just wishes that they would have been in a position for her to go back to work sooner but they just weren't.

Having Phil's wife work outside of the farmed made a

big difference and helped keep the farm going. He is more than just a little grateful to his beloved wife. For the last fifteen months the farm has been bringing more money. Phil and his wife were feeling more hope for the farm than they had felt in a long time. Frustratingly there were a couple of major farm projects that needed to be done for so long that couldn't be postponed any longer. These projects needed more cash so Phil took the night security job joining about half of the family farmers in the United States who have to have a second job.

For Phil and his wife the money from both of their outside jobs has taken a huge burden off of their shoulders. It is helping them get through the lean times. When equipment breaks down Phil has the money to get it repaired. He still doesn't have a lot of money to cover the cost for replacement of the equipment that he knows is going to need to be replaced soon. He just hopes that he can get more time out of each of the equipment.

For Phil keeping his farm is more than just a real estate or business concern. Farming is a way of life. He feels like somehow farming brings the best out in people. He is convinced that farmers are the best most wholesome people in the world. He knows one thing for sure that farmers helping farmers is a given. They do it without thinking, it's just done. If Phil needs help on the farm he has friends who farm who will drop everything and come to his aid. Phil can't think of many other people as a group that will help each other. Phil is a shy man who when he is away from the farm feels like a fish out of water. Even as he feels that way if a farmer is within shouting distance he can have something to talk about. It doesn't matter if the farmer he is talking to is one he hadn't met until then he can still have something to talk about. Not only that but by the time they part they will be fast friends. Phil believes that God was the first farmer. He created the Garden of Eden. It just doesn't get better than that.

Every day Phil hears of and knows farmers who have reached the end, have tried everything they can to save their farms but they simply cannot find any more money and the banks won't help them. These poor farmers finally have had to give up their farms. He knows of few things sadder than someone who was born to be a farmer having to walk away from their farm. Those that have to walk away become broken and are never the same. Phil never wants that to happen to his family and will do everything he can to keep that from happening.

Sometimes heroes save people, other times heroes work to save a way of life. Every time we go to a grocery store we see the results of heroes, the fruits of their labor. When we purchase our food we rarely think about the heroes who work long hours, fighting all kinds of weather including drought, heat and cold or the huge effort and sacrifices made by those living on small farms most that have been passed down from father to father even father to daughter for generations. We are in the midst of heroes and those who produce our food most defiantly are wearing blue jeans.

*The farms in the United States are the most productive food producers in the world. According to the United States Department of Agriculture over 1.3 million farms are operations where the owner is not looking to make a living from farming. This leaves only about 900,000 US farms that are able to provide a full time income for farmers and their families. About half of all family farmers have to work outside the farm to support their farms. Even at that according to Sustainabletable.com, every week 330 farmers are forced to leave their farms.*

# CARING

# HEROES FOR EACH OTHER

JOE WAS FORTY years old. He did not know what month or even what day he was born; all he knew was what year he was born in. He was raised in an orphanage for boys in Santa Barbara, California. His orphanage had their own school for children; grades first through seventh. Joe began school in first grade at the age of eight, and was already bigger and stronger than most of the other boys. Those in charge of the orphanage determined that he wasn't as smart as he was strong. A few days after Joe began school, he was sent to help the gardeners and repairmen doing any activity that required him to lift, pull, push, dig, and carry.

Joe grew stronger and taller each day that he was worked in the beautiful Santa Barbara sun. As long as Joe could remember, he always wanted a mother and father. Unfortunately, as he grew bigger and stronger, he became less and less attractive to potential parents who were looking to adopt a child from the orphanage. By age fifteen, with no one looking to adopt a six foot, two inch, very strong young man, he was told it was time for him to leave the orphanage. He was given five one dollar bills and a goodbye.

Joe was glad to leave the orphanage. The weather was warm, so for the first few days after he left the orphanage, he slept on the beach. He quickly found work helping build the break wall by Stearns Warf. His job was to carry huge boulders to plant in the sand, helping create the break wall. Joe lived in a time where there were plenty of jobs for strong men and could lift, but did not have any real career skills. After Joe finished working on the Break Wall, he found plenty of day labor jobs and a room at a Boarding House.

Joe was a gentle giant. He liked every one and no one ever saw him angry, though he was frequently sad. He had an almost childlike spirit, one that was innocent and full of wonder. It was a spirit rarely seen in a man the size of Joe. By the time Joe was twenty, almost everyone in Santa Barbara knew him, but few treated him seriously. He liked to hug and shake hands with almost anyone and everyone he met. He was so big and strong that when he shook hands and hugged, he overwhelmed people, especially women. Joe had very few friends, because he tried too hard to get them.

Joe could swim as long as he could remember. When he wasn't working, he was swimming. He liked to swim in the ocean, especially deep water. In Santa Barbara, he had to swim a ways out before he could swim out to the deep water. He would sometimes swim near swimmers who were struggling, and without any formal training, Joe instinctively knew how to rescue the swimmers.

By age seventeen, Joe had rescue his twelfth swimmer and just brought her to the beach. He was calming her down by the time the head life guard ran out to Joe to try to help. He found out that Joe didn't need any help, as he saw that the swimmer was wrapped in a blanket and taking deep breaths by the time he had reached them. He paused for a minute, and then offered Joe a part time life guard position on the East Beach. He accepted the job and did it well for fifty-three years, only taking two years off to serve in the navy shoveling coal into the furnaces of a ship that went back and forth across the Atlantic from the United States to Great Britain.

Joe had a way of keeping busy in his daily life. When he wasn't at the beach, he helped build houses, but never doing skilled labor. He usually worked at the building sites lifting boards, cement, shingles, and doing clean up. When he wasn't working on house building, he helped clear land so that others could build later. He was sought after to work on clearing land, because with his broad shoulders and strong arms, and when given a rake, shovel, and ax; he could clear more chaparral, tumble weeds, and trees than any team of three men. If a hole or holes were needed to be dug fast, Joe was the man everyone wanted.

Joe was a handsome man that most women, even married women, gave a second or a third glance at. He should have had lots of girlfriends, but Joe was painfully shy around women. Around men, he felt like he was judged by what kind of a man he was. What he did was more important than how he talked, or even what he said. Joe knew he sounded ignorant when he spoke, because he knew he was ignorant. When he thought of the book learning he had acquired in his life, he realized how little he actually had. He learned the alphabet in the few days that he was in the orphanage. By working his jobs he recognized numbers one through one hundred but couldn't think of much else that he knew, and this made him insecure around women.

Joe met Mary when he was doing a big clean up job on Cabrillo Street. Mary was an elegant and brilliant woman, but she was not beautiful. She was as close to ugly as any woman in Santa Barbara was. At sixty-four, she was long past the prime she never had, but she was a woman everyone noticed and everyone respected.

Mary had been a career woman at a time when not many women had careers. Mary worked for an insurance company for thirty-two years. When she wasn't working and in church, she was in the middle of her flowers. She had a pretty little three bedroom house in the nearby town of Carpentaria. Her house was nice, but her flower gardens that surrounded her home were known as the prettiest gardens outside of the Childs Estate, near East Beach in Santa Barbara. Mary was proud of the job she did for the insurance company and with her flower gardens. For Mary, life would be good if she wasn't so lonely.

When Joe and Mary met, they literally bumped in to each other. Joe had just finished carrying a load of broken boards to the curb. Mary was on her way to the library and carrying five books that she had borrowed and was returning. Mary's attention was drawn to the handsome man carrying scrap materials to the curb, and Joe's attention was drawn to the lady the books rather than to where he was walking. There was a fig tree growing near where Joe and Mary were, and a few of its roots were about four inches above the grass.

Joe had been walking around and over the roots since he began the job, but his attention was on Mary. They both tripped over the same root at the same time. It could be said that they fell for each other. Joe put his arm around Mary to keep her from falling. Mary let out a little scream and then said, "This is nice, but we haven't been formally introduced yet." Joe turned several shades of red and, after several tries, managed to say, "I'm sorry." Mary said, "All will be forgiven if you buy me a cup of coffee after you walk with me to return my books."

For the next six months, Joe and Mary shared a lot of coffees together, took a lot of walks on the beach together, and gardened together many times. After a while, they began to talk about getting married. Joe's few friends were against it because Mary was twenty-four years older than Joe, and for most men, she was not easy to look at. They told him that if he did marry her, the marriage wouldn't last long because Mary was so old. Mary's many friends were against her marrying Joe, because they thought Joe was not very bright. Mary was sure that Joe was intelligent, just an uneducated man. She even taught him to read from the King James Version of the Bible. Joe and Mary planned their wedding in spite of what their friends thought.

Joe and Mary were married on Mary's sixty-fifth birthday. Contrary to what people thought would happen, they had thirty wonderful years together, and for those years, they were the happiest couple in Santa Barbara. It was said that no matter how bad the weather was, as far as Joe and Mary were concerned, every day was a sunny day. Mary died three days after their thirtieth anniversary, when she was ninety-five years of age. The thirty years they spent together was the happiest years of their lives.

Being loved is among the greatest of all human needs. Although Joe and Mary led good lives on their own, they were not complete without love. A hero is one who reaches out; one who has a tender heart. Love is the greatest of all selfless acts. As a life guard, Joe was a hero many times, but his heroic acts were because of a universal love for mankind. When Joe reached out to Mary, and her to him, they became heroes of the highest order. Joe and Mary were heroes for each other.

In the memories of many, Joe and Mary can still be seen working among their flowers, Joe in his blue jeans and Mary in her blue jean skirt. Joe and Mary were heroes in blue jeans. Heroes are brilliant and even have challenges learning. We are in the midst of heroes, even in our neighborhoods, all we have to do is to look for them.

# Suddenly a Stroke

A NGUS IS A big man and a man's man. He is six foot four inches tall. He weighs two hundred twenty-two pounds and all of if it muscle. At first glance he looks mean and scary, until he smiles. His smile is as warm as the summer sun. He is in as good a shape as any man of fifty-two years of age out to be in.

As big as he is he is one of the kindest, well liked men in Wabasha County. He married a girl who was almost a foot shorter than he was. The woman he married, Candace, was only 5'5" tall and weighed just one hundred five pounds. After a few years of marriage they began their family with the first of three daughters.

Angus lives in one of the most beautiful parts of the country and he has a real eye for beauty. He especially likes the outdoors. Until recently and as long as he can remember he would wake up before the sun rose so that he could enjoy the beauty of the sunrise. He always thought that if he could begin each day seeing a sunrise it would set the tone for the rest of the day. No matter how difficult things were all he had to do was to think of the sunrise and his day would be better. As often as he could he would take the time to enjoy sunsets as well. What a beautiful way to end the day he always thought, especially if his family was enjoying the sunset with him.

When Angus wasn't working he was an amateur landscape artist. His paintings are quite good but he has never sold any for money. Not because he couldn't. If he had chosen to sell his paintings they would have sold well. Anyone who saw his paintings wanted to own them. For him he didn't paint for money but for love, love of each scene that he painted. His paintings were meant to be gifts for those he cared for, to share the beauty he enjoyed enough to paint. He wished he had more time to paint as every time he was outdoors he saw landscapes he really wished he could paint.

When he wasn't painting he was fishing. To Angus seeing a fish so sleek jumping out of the water with the sun glistening off its scales in the pristine beauty of a lake, river or stream was a magnificent experience. He was a good hunter since he loved just being in the woods so much so that he took everything in. Angus saw the little details that most hunters and game wardens would miss. He was able to see where deer and elk had recently been or might even still be. For that reason alone he always got his limit.

He and his family frequently went camping. He loved nature so much that he was always reading and researching the world around him. Every time his family camped he would take them on nature walks sharing what he knew with those he loved the best. Camping created warm memories and visions of swimming, hiking, riding four wheelers, motorcycles, jet skis and snowmobiles in everyone's minds eye.

Angus enjoys beauty away from the woods as well. His home is in the country on top of a hill on eight acres of farm/ timber land. Brightly colored flowers are everywhere. He has a small vegetable garden, some blueberry bushes and some fruit trees for his family near the house. Inside of his ranch style house are all kinds of art. He loves music. His beloved antique upright piano has a place of honor in his living room. There are two guitars in their cases leaning up against the wall near the piano. There is a book shelf full of music books across from the piano.

In their family room it is obvious that Angus enjoys movies. He has a lot of DVDs of all categories of movies. There are three well used computers and a television Angus was given by his older brother. He and his wife have frequent barbecues where he is in charge of the grill and entertainment. It is also when he gives away most of his paintings. No one who has ever been to one of his barbecues leave hungry, sad or disappointed.

Angus enjoys going to live theater and concerts. He

won't miss a rodeo or an air show if it is within a two hour ride. He has gone to county and state fairs since he was a little fellah. He has a special interest in these fairs because he is a County Agricultural Agent. He works with farmers as a resource for them to turn to when they need help especially when times are tough and around his county times have been tough for a lot of years.

Angus has never smoked or done drugs. On occasion he has a glass or two of red wine. For Angus drinking wine is more for the experience than it is for anything. He likes how all of his senses can take part in the sipping a glass of wine. He just doesn't feel the need to experience it very often or to drink more than one glass usually or two at the most. To be sociable he sometimes nurses a bottle of beer for a whole night if he is at a friend's house or if a one of those he invites to his barbecues bring beer. He had never grown fond of beer but he considers himself to be a good ol' boy and as far as he knows good ol' boys drink beer and so does he, even if it is just for appearance sake.

About a year ago Angus hugged his wife and shared with her how much he had been enjoying his family. He expressed to her how she has grown more and more beautiful each year that he has been married to her. He told her of how proud he was of their three girls. That he really had noticed how beautiful the women in his life are. He told her that he had four surprises for her. What he had done was not as good as he had hoped as it was something he had never attempted to do before. He wished he had done it sooner and more often. He hoped that she would like the gifts. He handed her four packages in brown wrapped paper.

Candace fingers trembled as she opened the first one because something told her that these gifts were to be very special indeed. The first gift that she opened was a portrait of their oldest daughter. It was so beautiful and looked so life like that she expected to hear her daughter's voice coming out as she looked at it. What really astonished her was that the smile on the portrait was so beautiful, almost like a Mona Lisa type smile. She opened up the other two packages. They were just as beautiful as the portrait of their other daughter was. The smiles on their portraits were just as sweet as the smile on their sister's portrait.

When Candace opened up the last package and saw that the package was a portrait of her, her eyes filled with tears. Her portrait was her at her best, even better than her best. Candace had never been given a gift that she loved more. She hugged Angus tightly and her tears came down in a torrent. She told him that she had never seen portraits that were more beautiful, that she loved them and that she just knew the girls would love them too. She was right the girls did love them. The girls asked Candace if the portraits could be hung in the living room. Angus and Candace hung them right then and there. Angus couldn't be happier that his family liked their portraits so much. Candace thanked Angus again and then said that she just wished that Angus had painted a self-portrait. He thought that idea was a good one and he would begin tomorrow afternoon.

The day he was to begin painting his self-portrait began with one of the most beautiful sunrises that he had ever seen. Before he left for work he found a photo he could use to paint his portrait from. He gathered up his easel, his paints, a new canvas and the photo placing them on the floor next to his desk in his home office. His work day had him driving out to the prettiest farms through the most magnificent scenery in any part of the country. At lunch he found a spot by a lake that had a loon fishing on it, six ducks swimming and a two bald eagles putting on an air show to his delight. The air was crisp though not cold. The mountains in the background had their first real dusting of snow and the leaves on the trees all around had really put on their fall display more vibrant than he had ever remembered seeing.

His day at work was as good a day as he had ever remembered in eighteen years of being a County Agricultural Agent. As he got out of his truck he was whistling a song from his childhood. He came in to the house hugged and kissed his wife, changed out of his uniform greeted his three daughters, enquired about their school, signed a few papers for them and told them that he loved them.

It was a good thing that Angus came home when he did because within fifteen minutes of his arrival Candace and the girls were on their way out to piano lessons and a Girl Scout meeting. They would be back in three hours. Candace had just put his dinner in the microwave oven. It would be done in forty-two minutes. All Angus had to do was to take it out open the cover and eat it. They were going to grab some burgers on their way home. One weakness that Angus had was that he was not a good cook. He never pretended that he was. Candace was an exceptional cook and always made sure that if she was out Angus had good food to eat. Having a wife like Candace made Angus feel like life just couldn't get any better.

After saying goodbye to his beloved family Angus went to his office to retrieve his painting gear. He set up his easel on the front porch facing the mountains in the distance found his painting chair sat down on the chair, took out a brush began to dip his brush in the paint when suddenly he couldn't see. One moment he could see clearly then everything went completely dark. There wasn't any light or maybe just a little light. At first he thought he was just tired so he rubbed his eyes and tried to see. For a few seconds after he rubbed his eyes he thought maybe he was wrong, he could see shadows or at least some shadows. He rubbed his eyes again and then there was absolutely no light. It reminded him of the time he visited Mammoth Caves in Kentucky and they turned out the lights. Angus had no idea what was going on with him. He only knew that suddenly he was in total darkness. He was very afraid and began to panic.

Angus fought to keep the feeling of panic from over taking him knowing that panicking would simply make whatever was wrong with him worse. To limit his panic he did an inventory of his senses to determine what the damage was. He first checked on his reasoning. He did a quick recall check. He was relieved to know that he could recall his personal information like what was his own name, how old he was his wife's name and daughters' names. Angus knew their ages too. He knew how long he was married. He knew who he worked for and for how long. He knew his address, his telephone numbers and several of his family members' telephone numbers. He could do basic math operations in his head and more. Angus checked his fine motor skills and was able to hold the paint brush, move his fingers arms and legs from a sitting position. Everything but his eyes were in good working order as far as he could tell.

Angus was glad to find out that the only thing he had lost was his vision, though that was a major loss. He did not have time to grieve because he knew that his best chance to fix whatever was wrong was for him to be seen by a doctor as soon as possible. Angus guessed that his family had left no more than fifteen minutes earlier so they wouldn't be back for at least two hours. His best hope for help would be for him to call 911. Unfortunately he had left his cell phone on the coffee table just inside the front door near the door leading to the porch.

For Angus to get to his cell phone he knew that he would have to walk in total darkness behind his chair into the living room. As he sat on his chair he knew where the outside was and where his living room and cell phone were. The living room was behind his chair. Angus stood up, took two steps forward and became disoriented. He wasn't sure where to go. For a moment he stood still not sure what to do next. He thought that maybe he should just go sit back down but where was his chair? Was he still standing up? He was pretty sure that he was. If he was just standing not doing anything it wasn't doing him any good. He took a few more steps but this confused him enough for panic to set in once again. Angus had to keep moving. He took a deep breath and attempted another step but as he did he heard a sudden noise nearby and turned towards the sound. Unfortunately his foot was at the edge of the porch. The step took him beyond the edge which caused him to fall. He felt the sensation of falling just before his head and shoulder hit the bottom step of the porch. He lay motionless but no one was there to notice.

As Candace and the girls got in to their car after the piano lessons, Candace got a bad feeling about Angus. Instead of going to the Girl Scout meeting and a burger, Candace pointed the car towards home driving as fast as she could. As they got close to the house the four of them saw Angus lying on the ground by the porch and he didn't seem to be moving. Candace slammed on her brakes, threw open the door and ran to Angus calling out his name. He didn't respond. When she got to him she saw that he was bleeding from a head wound. She made sure the girls stayed far enough away to not panic and had one call 911 and to tell them to hurry. She was so afraid for him but noticed that even though he was unconscious he was breathing. The ambulance arrived within ten minutes. The emergency medical technicians who arrived gave a quick check of his vital signs to make sure that Angus was breathing OK as well as administered first aid to the head wound and a good sized bump on his head. They also immobilized his shoulder since they suspected he had a shoulder injury. They determined that his injuries were severe enough for them to take Angus to the hospital. By the time Angus was placed in the hospital it was two hours and seventeen minutes since his vision loss.

Two hours and twenty-seven minutes after Angus lost his vision he was brought into the Emergency Room at the hospital. His head wound was cleaned up and stitched. The bump on Angus's head was examined and x-rayed. He was beginning to become awake but was still disoriented. The clock ticked along. Two hours and forty-eight minutes had passed since he lost his vision. Angus's disorientation began to clear up enough to answer questions that the doctors and nurses asked him. It has been two hours and fifty-three minutes after he lost his vision before he finally shared with the doctors, nurses and his wife that soon after he sat down to do his self-portrait, he suddenly lost his sight. That was the reason he fell.

Four hours and fifty-three minutes after Angus lost his vision and two hours after he told the doctors that he couldn't see Angus's doctors gave him a diagnosis for his sudden blindness as an Occipital Stroke causing Cortical Blindness. He was told that his eye functions were still intact but their processing was damaged. The good news was that his stroke did not affect any other part of his brain. The bad news was twofold: first they had a three hour window from when his stroke began for the best results for his treatment and the window had past. The second was that the damage done to his eyes were permanent and that it was unlikely that he would regain very much, if any of vision.

The doctor noted that his blood pressure was high so prescribed some medicine and put him on a strict diet. His doctor also referred him to an occupational therapist to help him learn how to live without being able to see. His doctor decided to have him spend the night at the hospital so that they could finish running a few more tests and so that they could monitor his head injury for a few hours. Angus always a gentleman thanked the doctors and nurses in the Emergency Room for their care.

After the doctor left and Angus was moved to the room where he would spend the night. Candace and the girls went with him and stayed a little while. Angus could hear the girls yawn. He knew that they must be exhausted. He suggested to Candace that they go home so that that they could get some rest for school the next day. Candace asked him if he was going to be OK. Angus said, "How could I not? I will be checked and rechecked all night long to see if I am OK. I know I won't really get rest until I come home tomorrow."

Candace said, "You are right. The girls need their sleep. I'll drive the girls to school early so I can be with you sooner tomorrow, k? Honey it's going to be OK. You must be devastated but I just know that everything will get better. I am not sure how but I know that it will." She paused a moment and spoke again, "I'll tell you this much, I would rather have the man I love to hold and to tell him how much I love him even if he is blind rather than just memories of that wonderful man. You lost a part of you but it isn't the best part. The best part of you is your heart." Angus could feel Candace's tears falling and could hear that his daughters were crying too.

Angus wanted to say something reassuring to them all but the best he could say was, "I love you, see you tomorrow." He just couldn't express what he wanted to say. His emotions for the moment were simply too deep to express.

After his beloved family left Angus became overwhelmed with emotions. For most of his life he was not a man who thought much about emotions. He felt what he felt when he felt. He showed his emotions to his family and in his paintings but he was rarely aware of strong feelings as he was now.

The first emotion was that of gratitude. He was thankful that he was still alive so that he could feel the love of his family. He was even more thankful that he was given more time day to really love them back more than he had before the stroke.

As much as he felt grateful, he also felt grief. All of the beauty in the world that he loved seeing so much was ripped away in a moment and he didn't even have a chance to say good bye. When he felt grief he also felt guilt. Guilt didn't waste a lot of time hitting him. It came as soon as he began to grieve for the loss of his eyesight. He had so much to be thankful for, especially his family. He knew that the love of his family was unconditional even if he was blind. He also felt he should be thankful that his stroke wasn't much worse. He knew of folks who had strokes that affected their thinking and their communication. Still the overwhelming feeling of grief seemed to envelop him.

As grief enveloped him it brought with it the last emotion that of fear. How was he going to keep his job now that he is blind? How would he look after and protect his family. Taking care of his family was a high priority in his life. When he could see he never thought of how much he relied on his eyes when it came to taking care of his family. Now he would have to use his ears to listen better than he had ever listened in his life. Would his family, friends and people who he works with treat him differently? He didn't want that to happen but it probably would. Would people pity him? Not a chance--he wouldn't let them.

He could think away his fears. He suspected Candace was right that things would work out but grief over his loss was something else. His grief was selfish he knew but it was real and crashed over him like ocean waves pushing him deeper and deeper in to a sadness that he had never known before, bringing him to the edge of despair.

As he thought about his lost vision it occurred to Angus that he probably enjoyed what he saw in life more than almost anyone he knew. He thought that even as old as he was he had probably seen more sunrises and sunsets than most people see in their entire lives. He knew that not many people had the kind of job that he had where they could see as many wonders as he did going from farm to farm. As a painter observing the little things was part of being artist. Angus remembered how much he enjoyed seeing the vibrant contrasting colors along with the dramatic images that is so much a part of nature. He enjoyed hunting and fishing and all that went in to both. All of those moments were gone forever for Angus and he grieved for his loss.

That night was one of the longest nights of his life. It was the first time that he had ever allowed himself the luxury of self-pity. He was understandably grieving but his grieving had turned into self-pity. It felt like he hadn't slept at all that night but eventually he fell in to a troubled sleep. At home Candace didn't sleep well in her bed that night either, grieving for her best friend and husband. She would have rather been with her husband that night but her girls needed reassurance that everything would be OK and she knew that Angus needed time to come to terms with his blindness. She couldn't do that for him. That was something that he had to do by himself, alone.

When Candace arrived at Angus's room she found him asleep with his face close to the wall. He had a look of exhaustion of one who had gone through a hard battle and he was sleeping a troubled sleep. When he woke up he reached out and gave his wife a long hug. As he hugged her he said, "You know I am not blind when I dream. I still see beauty in my dreams and I dreamed of you when I was dreaming last night.

Candace asked, "Rough night?

Angus replied, "Yep rough night but the sun is going to rise again. I will still have my rough times but I will get through them. I spent most of last night feeling bad for what my stroke stole from me. I stayed awake a long time but when I did fall asleep the dreams I had helped me to understand that my stroke ended one chapter of my life and forced open another door. What you told me before you left helped me more after I had time to reflect on things. Your words helped me so much." Candace held him close. Angus said, "You know the hardest part of being blind suddenly is the blackness feels so lonely. Your hug eases that loneliness." For a few special moments it was just Angus and Candace... it was enough.

Angus heard a sound outside his hospital room. It was his boss. His boss said, "Candace called to tell me about your stroke. Is there any chance that you will ever be able to see again?"

Angus said, "We have been told that it is highly unlikely."

His boss said, "You are my friend first and foremost, my employee next. The thing is you are not just my employee. You are the best I have. You really know farming and our farmers trust you. You still have a job and you better not even consider quitting."

"You still want me to work even though I am blind?" Angus asked.

His boss said, "I just told you I did. You can still use a computer. Before you went blind you typed without looking at the key board didn't you?"

"I did," Angus said.

"I just ordered software that will say what you type so you can type your regular reports. I have also taken the liberty to find someone to teach you to read Braille. I am paying for your lessons, a Braille embosser and some reference books in Braille since you will need them for your job." Angus fighting emotions told his boss how grateful he was for his friendship and his willingness to keep him on the job.

One thought occurred to Angus. He asked his boss what he was going to do about seeing the farmers since he could no longer drive. His boss told him that he just hired another front office person full time but until Angus had his stroke he wasn't sure what he was going to have the person do half of the day when her office duties were done. He said she was already so good at her job that he didn't want to lose her. Now she could drive him to his farmers. Angus asked for time off work to learn Braille. His boss agreed and wanted him to use two weeks of his sick time to get used to being blind.

Angus was kept an extra day in the hospital. He was given a cane and shown how to use it. They had him practice walking the halls with the cane without stumbling too much. He was instructed on the fine points of dressing, eating and shaving without the benefit of eye sight. After some messy first attempts at eating and shaving he caught on quickly enough. When Angus was released from the hospital he felt a feeling of accomplishment that he hadn't felt in a long time. When he did go home he was able to get manage pretty well though he did occasionally fall. For Angus, Candace and his girls it was good for him to be back at home. A few days after he got home Candace had a surprise for him. She had gone to the National Library Services for the Blind & Handicapped and ordered books and magazines that he could listen to. This helped his dark world seem less dark for him.

Even with the familiarity of his home, adjusting to a dark world was quite an adjustment but with some extra effort Angus was able to do most things that he needed and wanted to do around the house. Support from family and friends made the adjustment for Angus easier. There came a day soon after Angus came home that Candace insisted he accompany her to town to shop. He thought it was too soon. For Candace getting him out away from home was something he had to do sooner rather than later.

When Candace and Angus went shopping he was able to do quite well getting around moving his cane back and forth the way he was taught. So many people stopped and visited with them. Angus could tell that some who he had known all of his life pitied him while others even in their short visit treated him differently than before his stroke. He remembered thinking about that possibility in the hospital but now he felt like pitying him and treating him differently than before wasn't his problem but was the problem of the people who pitied him and treated him differently. He would spend more time with people who treated him as they always did.

When Angus went back to work some weeks later he could not remember when he had enjoyed his job more. Before coming back he had learned to read Braille and his boss, true to his word, had installed the software called 'A Screen Reader' that audibly read whatever was on the screen. The first days were exhausting trying to remember where things were, listening to the computer as he typed, and going out to visit the farmers he helped. The young lady who was his driver came from a family he knew well. He grew up with her mother and uncle, knew her daddy, grandparents and even her great grandparents. She had a maturity that was beyond her years and seemed to sense when he needed help and when she should back off a bit.

For Angus some good things came out of being blind. One of the best things was that he learned to be a much better listener than he ever was before. For his wife and daughters especially, but to everyone else as well who needed or wanted to talk to him, no matter what he was doing when they wanted to visit he always stopped what he was doing to give them his complete attention. He no longer listened to them with half an ear. Along with that he was able to enjoy the beauty he could hear much more than he ever could before. Birds singing, the many sounds of farm animals, music in all forms and even the symphony of silence all were moments of beauty that he had never taken the time to enjoy before his stroke. As Angus learned to adjust to his blindness he became more patient with those around him and a kinder man reaching out to those who needed a hand. If he couldn't help he knew those who could. Candace said that her husband was a good man before his stroke. He became a better man after his stroke.

Life still had its down moments. For weeks he could not go near his art supplies. Even thinking about his art made him sad. One day a few months after his stroke Angus had an artist friend visit him. As they visited awhile his friend asked Angus if he was still painting. Angus said, "I haven't painted since the day before my stroke."

His friend asked, "Why not?"

"I'm blind. How can I paint when I am blind," Angus asked him.

"Just paint from your memory and add a touch of imagination," his friend said.

Angus asked, "Do you really think that it is possible?"

His friend said, "Not only is it possible but you need to do it." For two days Angus would go to his art supplies and touch them one at a time then would leave and come back later only to do the same thing. On the third day he asked one of his daughters to place each paint color in a specific spot on his pallet. Three times he asked her to tell him exactly where each color was. After the third time he told her where each color was. He had memorized the color placement exactly how it was. In minutes he began to paint again something he thought he would never do. When asked what the painting was he would only say it was a gift for Candace. In a few weeks his painting was done and he presented the painting to Candace. It was his self-portrait. Candace burst in to tears and told him that the painting was as good a painting as he had ever done.

Angus reached a point where a guide dog would be helpful especially on the farms he visited so he contacted Guide Dogs for the Blind, filled out an application and after a bit of a wait he was accepted in to the program. He and his dog went through a rigorous program that made life easier for him.

His life had become good. There were still things Angus missed about seeing like sunrises and sunsets, driving a car or hunting but Angus believes that in life nothing happens by chance. He knows his vision loss was for a reason. He feels like losing his vision has helped refine his spirit.

Being blind limits a person less and less. He found out he could play golf using balls that had a beeper in it, join a softball league for people who are blind and so much more. Angus was also thinking of taking up skiing. One of the nearby mountain ski resorts had a program where with the help of a guide, people who are blind could alpine and Nordic ski. Angus recently found out that there are four states where hunters who are blind can hunt and he is looking in to it.

Attitude is everything. It has been said that a skipper on a ship is considered a hero if no matter how bad the storm he keeps the rudder steady. Heroes don't always jump in front of cars or rescue drowning dogs. Sometimes a hero is a hero because he keeps going even in the most severe storm. We are in the midst of heroes, about five million of them.

*According to the US News and World Report, strokes are the third-leading cause of death in the United States behind heart disease and cancer, killing about 275,000 people a year. On average, someone in the United States has a stroke about once every forty-five seconds, for a total of about 700,000 and people per year. Five million stroke survivors live in the United States today.*

# Roommates

DANIEL AND DAVID are roommates. They have a lot in common. They both have an intellectual or developmental disability. They share a two bedroom apartment. They share household chores even cooking their meals. They are best friends. They are six months apart in age. David is twenty-eight. Daniel is twenty eight and a half. Daniel likes to tell everyone that he is older so he gets to make the decisions around the apartment like what cartoons they see first on Saturday mornings. They like different cartoons but since they are best friends they enjoy watching their favorite cartoons together.

They both work for the same new and used car lot washing cars. It is a big car lot with lots of cars that need to be washed. If the weather gets bad they can wash the same car several times. They both work hard though they sometimes get wet more than they need to. They work on different cars but they both focus on making sure that the cars they wash are spotless. Their boss is very pleased with their work.

David is taller than Daniel. He does windows better than anyone. It is not hard to know which cars he has washed by simply looking at the windows. They are so clean they almost look like there isn't any glass in them. Daniel cleans any kind of wheel better than anyone. He takes time to make each wheel sparkle when he is done. In the ten years since they began to work there Daniel has only missed two days when his mother died and David has only missed four days when he had pneumonia.

Pay day is always exciting for both men. After they get paid they always sit down with a helper who helps them pay their bills, sharing the costs equally and fairly. The helper then takes them to buy groceries. They get state help with groceries so not much of their pay goes to buying groceries. Their helper insists that they buy healthy foods and has taught them how to make a great many quick and easy healthy meals and snacks. Daniel likes chocolate and David likes soda. Their helper has told them if they want to buy soda and candy the money to pay for them must come from their pay. He helps them each budget for their candy and soda.

Once a week, usually on Fridays after work, they eat out at an 'all you can eat' restaurant because both agree that you don't have to wait long to eat. After they eat they will go to a movie unless there is nothing good to see and that happens sometimes. If there isn't anything good to see then they either rent a movie or just watch cable. They have cable and Daniel will tell anyone who will listen to him that cable has a kajillion channels. David says that is not a real number but he does admit that cable has a lot of channels.

Both men are proud Special Olympians. David is a winter and summer Special Olympian. In the winter he cross country skis in short races. In the summer he is on the swim team where he competes in free style and breast stroke swimming competitions. Daniel only participates in summer Special Olympics in shot put and 400k walking events. David has tried many times to get Daniel to do winter Special Olympics but Daniel always says, "I wash cars in the cold because that's my job. I don't like cold if I am not at my job. I would rather stay home and watch cartoons."

When they have free time they both help out at the Animal shelter, walking dogs mostly, but sometimes do other things like clean out cages. They both love animals and know that they can't have an animal in their apartment so volunteering at the animal shelter gives them a chance to love animals--kitties and dogs mostly. Everyone at the shelter loves to have them helping there and they feel like they are doing something good.

Both men are proud of what they have accomplished. They both live pretty much independently with just a little help. They both have paying jobs that they like and are good at. Both men volunteer and are athletic though admittedly David is a bit more athletic than Daniel is. Daniels stomach has stretched some larger than it was when he was eighteen where as David is just as thin as he was when he was eighteen maybe a little thinner even. Both men are loved by their family, people they work with and their community. Life just couldn't get much better than that.

There is something they never get used to though. There are always some who make fun of them. David says, "Some people talk about us in front of us like we are too stupid to know. We know we know and it hurts."

Daniel adds to the conversation by saying, "Yeah we are just like everybody else. We learn slower than lots of people but we can learn a lot of things even if it takes longer. I get so excited when I learn things. So does David. I bet we like learning more than most people do because it is so hard for us to learn. When we do learn it's like winning a race. Besides David knows more about music than anyone I know."

David beams and says, "He is right you know. I can tell you every song that was ever written and who has performed it since 1963. You can check on me if you want to."

Heroes always go the extra mile. David and Daniel go more than just the extra mile. There isn't any part of their life that is easy yet they always try and they never give up. The Special Olympic motto is 'Let me win but if I cannot win let me be brave in the attempt'. It is not just for the athletic events and venues for these two men or men and women like them but goes far beyond the athletic arena to their work and home life. Heroes aren't always brilliant but they always have heart. We are in the midst of heroes like Daniel and David, over four million of them who every day go the extra mile not because they want to but because for them there is no other option.

*According to ARC there are an estimated 4.6 million Americans who have an intellectual or developmental disability. In-*

tellectual disability is a disability that occurs before age 18. People with this disability experience significant limitations in two main areas: 1) intellectual functioning and 2) adaptive behavior. These limitations are expressed in the person's conceptual, social and practical everyday living skills

According to Wikipedia, Special Olympics is the world's largest sports organization for children and adults with disabilities, providing year-round training and competitions to more than 4 million athletes in 170 countries. Special Olympics competitions are held every day, all around the world—including local, national and regional competitions, adding up to more than 53,000 events a year.

# Heroes for the Moment

HOWARD IS FORTY-THREE years old. He is developmentally disabled. He is unable to talk but uses head nods, shakes, facial expressions and a book of photos with a word under each photo that is used as a communication tool. He works part time for a sporting goods store sweeping mopping and taking out the trash in the store.

Howard is proud to be able to keep his room clean at the house he lives at, that he always dresses neatly, cleanly shaved and hair always neatly brushed. He is proud that he has a job and that because of that he has spending money to see a movie once a week but he is proudest of being a Special Athlete.

He has been in Special Athletics for thirty-five years. He is involved in Winter Games and in Summer Games. He enjoys Winter Games but his favorite games are Summer Games. He participates in short walking races. Whenever he races he never finishes lower than third place mostly takes second place but sometimes wins first place. He is proud of his medals and ribbons. He wears the ribbons most of the time but when he doesn't, he always has two or three ribbons in his pockets to show anyone he meets.

As far as anyone knows Howard has never had a girlfriend. He hasn't ever really needed one. He has people who love and watch over him. That is enough for Howard.

Howard has been looking forward to Summer Games since the first day of practice some three months ago. He has slept well, eaten a big breakfast and is ready to race. It is a fifty meter walking race. His race is called. Along with his coach he checks in. He is assigned lane three. Lane three is his favorite lane. His eyes are focused on the official with the starting gun as he always does just before a race starts that is until Jane checks in and is assigned lane two. He takes his eye off the official with the starting gun and focuses completely on Jane. Jane looks back at Howard and their eyes lock.

Jane and Howard have a lot in common even if they don't know it. Jane is the same age as Howard. Like Howard Jane is unable to talk and unlike Howard she uses sign language to communicate. She also works part time but at a grocery store. Her job was to sweep, mop and empty trash cans. Like Howard she is a proud to be a Special Athlete. She participates in Winter and Summer Games like Howard does. She races in short walking races and has many first, second and third place but mostly second place medals and ribbons. She always carries at least one of her ribbons and one of her medals with her at all times even when she goes to bed except then she places her ribbons and medals by her pillow.

As far as anyone knows Jane has never had a boyfriend. She hasn't ever really needed one. She has people who love and watch over her. That is enough for Jane.

For whatever reason there are only two athletes in the race. The race is about to begin. One of the officials call out, "On Your Mark, get set, get set......." At this point usually get in position when they race but today the only two athletes Howard and Jane ignore the official they just look at each other. The gun goes off, the race is on. All the spectators near the race cheer Howard and Jane on but in spite of everyone's support Howard and Jane don't move, they just look at each other. The cheering becomes louder and the cry of go, go, go, go can be heard all around them. Still neither one of them will move. After five minutes of the two of them just gazing at each other Howard reaches his hand out towards Jane. Jane takes his hand and together they walk towards the finish line.

Howard and Jane finish the race together. They are both declared winners and both are given first place medals. In the few minutes since Howard's eyes met they knew love, unspoken all-encompassing love. Anyone who is at the race will always remember their act of love in its purest form. Neither athlete is willing to climb the podium to receive their medals or to let go of each other's hand so it is decided to award them their medals at the finish line that they have just crossed.

After their medals are awarded Howard and Jane give each other one final look and then stop holding hands. The games last four and half more days yet they never again hold hands or even glance at each other even the following two races they compete against each other in.

Howard and Jane have done something no other athlete in Special Athletics. They crossed the finish line holding hands. What they shared in the few moments of their race was something not everyone experiences in their lives, unconditional love.

Heroes are heroes because they care. It is the reason that they reach out to do the heroic acts that they do. How long does it take for heroic acts to occur? Sometimes it just takes a moment. Howard and Jane were heroes even if it was just for a moment. Having a disability does not prevent people from being heroes. The only limit in being a hero is attitude. We are in the midst of heroes we just need to look for them.

# BREAKING AWAY

DALE IS THIRTY-FIVE years old Texan, living in Washington State. He is a tall, thin man with wispy blond hair, which is usually hidden by his cowboy hat. He always wears faded blue jeans and a plaid cowboy shirt. He has piercing blue eyes that seem to look inside the heart of everyone he meets, making some curious and others very uncomfortable. His Texas drawl is a bit gravelly, coupled with his southern politeness. His "Howdy ma'am" or "Howdy sir" draws people to him, and even though people are drawn to him, he is careful who he talks to beyond the Texas greeting.

Dale works in a factory in production control. He is a liaison between engineering and manufacturing. He works hard and treats everyone he works with fairly. He is good at his job and the possibility of promotion is very real. His factory recently hired a new employee doing the same job Dale does; his name is Hal. After a week of observing Hal, Dale reaches the conclusion that Hal is making more than his share of mistakes, even for a new hire. It's not that Hal isn't trying; he is trying very hard, in fact, too hard. It is obvious that he cares about his job, but he is so afraid to make mistakes, that he makes more mistakes than he would have if he wasn't so worried.

Dale finds himself liking Hal, in spite of himself. Being the kind of man Dale is, he reaches out to help Hal get back on track. He makes sure that everyone at the factory knows that he is looking after Hal. He encourages Hal to slow down until he gets comfortable with his job, and it doesn't take long before Hal is doing his job well. One day, the factory employees were giving Hal a hard time, not doing the job the way it was suppose to be done. Hal became so upset that he yelled at the employees. A few of the employees yelled back and some openly laughed at him. As soon as Dale could, he came over to support Hal. Dale gave each employee a look that stopped them cold. There were mumbled apologies, and every employee that gave Hal a hard time got busy and fixed the problems that were made.

Dale said, "Because you yelled at the employees, you just showed them that you weren't anyone to be afraid of." Hal said, "They were not doing the job the way it was supposed to be done. They have packaged those parts at least a thousand times." Dale said, "You are right, they weren't doing the job right, but if you had quietly told them the same thing that you yelled at them about, they would have had reason to fear you. Did you know that when a career criminal kills someone, they never even change expression before during or after they kill?" Hal asked, "How would you know that?" Dale said, "Because I have six older brothers, all of them in prison back in Texas for murder."

Dale said, "Sit down Hal and let me tell you why I am up here in Washington State when I am Texas through and through." Hal sat down and Dale continued, "I am the youngest of seven brothers, and the only one not in prison. Only two of my brothers have any hopes of getting out. For generations, as far as I can go back, my family has been in and out of jail and prisons. My Poppa and Ma were in and out of prison when I was growing up. Whenever we had a school holiday, I was always going to visit one or the other of them and my brothers. My friends were all people who broke the law more than once. I spent time in prison for robbery, and they let me off after five years."

"While in prison, I had time to think about what I wanted in life and what I didn't want. I had all of the life of crime and prison that I could stomach. Outside of prison, I wasn't a gang member, so I wasn't forced to be a criminal. After I got out of prison, too many people knew about my family for me to get a full time job, and no matter how hard I tried not to, I was becoming more drawn into a life that I did not want. I realized the only way I was going to leave that life behind was to break away and go as far away from the life I knew as I could.

I put what little I had in a back pack, grabbed a sleeping bag, walked over to a truck stop, and hitched a ride. I was asked where I was going, I said as far as I could go. This trucker was going to Washington State, and when we got here, he asked me if I needed a job. I said I did, and he gave me the address of this factory and a name. I was given a chance to live an honest and honorable life, and I took it. I now have a nice house and am engaged to one of the ladies who works with us. I finally have the kind of life I wanted so badly back in prison.

Hal asked, "How was it that, after generations of people in your family that lived lives as criminals, you were able to pull away from the only life you knew?" Dale said, "It was either that or go back to prison. For me, to go back to prison meant death. I needed a change, and change takes courage. Take away the guns and knives, and you won't find many criminals with courage. The reason I am the first and so far only one in my family to leave a life of crime, is that I am the only one who found the courage to do so. I really wanted to break away from the life I knew, and the only way I could do that, was to reach inside of me to find the courage I desperately needed. It was there because I looked for it. Life is about choices, isn't it?"

It takes a real hero to break away from generations of bad behavior, no matter what the behavior is. Did Dale save a life or lives by breaking away from the example his family gave him? It can only be surmised, since his six brothers all were convicted of murder, that he was more likely than most people to commit murder. If the world was lucky, he might have only committed one murder. The actions that he took to break away from the history of criminal activities in his family made Dale a real hero. Heroes are all around us, even in the work place, we just have to look for them.

# And Then There Was One

L EE LEE GAVE Bubba a great bird-hunting dog, and he was very overjoyed. She was the best female dog in the litter, and Bubba liked female dogs, they were always easier to train somehow. His new dog was supposed to be just a bird dog, but later on, he found that she was a squirrel dog too. He found that out by accident. One day, while Bubba got ready to go hunting, he got his gun out of the cabinet and headed out the door. Before he could shut the door, she ran out and followed him. As he looked for squirrels, she stood completely still right beside him. Then, he pointed his gun at a squirrel and pulled the trigger. As soon as he pulled the trigger, she ran to where the squirrel was shot and brought it back to him.

Bubba loved that dog. He named her Annie, after his first wife. One day, a stray dog came in to Bubba's yard about the time Annie got out. For the first time in her life Annie refused to follow a command, even when Bubba threw a work boot at her. After a bit, Annie came back. Bubba had thought about neutering Annie at least five times before the stray came in to his yard, but Bubba was a bit on the lazy side. Plus, the veterinarian would take his beer money for taking care of Annie. He kept thinking that he would get Annie taken care of when the Animal Hospital had a sale, but they never did. Since he didn't spay Annie, it wasn't long before she had her first litter of puppies. She had six of them.

Bubba had no use for six mongrel puppies. The more he thought about the puppies, the angrier he became. Since he was lazy, he couldn't be bothered to find homes for the puppies or even call the pound. Not being very smart or caring, when the puppies were just four weeks old and not fully weaned from their mother, he emptied a beer case, gathered up all six puppies, and dumped them into the case ignoring the squeals and yips from the puppies. He then threw the box of puppies in to the back of his old Ford Pickup, opened up a bottle of beer, drank half of the bottle, got in to the pickup, and drove the puppies out into the country.

Bubba saw a clump of trees, about a mile from the nearest house, and thought that this would be as good a place as any to dump the dogs. So he pulled his pickup to the side of the road, threw the now empty beer bottle in to the back of the truck, and opened another one. He closed his eyes and drank the beer, almost in one gulp, then let that bottle fall beside the truck. He picked up the box of puppies, staggered to the nearest tree in the clump of trees, and dumped the puppies near it. The puppies cried and yipped in surprise and fear as they watched Bubba get into his truck with yet another beer in his hand and drive off down the road.

When Bubba got home, he staggered into his house and plopped down on his aptly named "Lazy Boy" chair. He took his remote and pointed it at his television, clicking until he found a channel where he could watch a game. It didn't matter what the game was, as long as it was a game. He sunk into a semi stupor caused by alcohol and laziness.

Bubba's cousin, Billy, walked in to the house and plopped himself down on the couch next to Bubba. No words were exchanged between the two for about seven minutes. Then they shared the usual southern polite greeting of, "Hey.", and then they were silent for another ten minutes or so. For no real reason, Bubba said, "Got rid of them puppies I had." Billy said, "Didn't see them when I came in. I saw Annie pacing and whimpering, but I didn't see the puppies, so I figured you did something with them. Did you kill them?" Bubba said. "Annie will get over them. I didn't kill them, too hot to kill them. Not that I didn't think about it. Remember Eula May's eight puppies she wanted to get rid of back a ways? I poisoned them. Problem with that was, it was messy and it took a while. So, these puppies, I just took out to the country and dumped them." Billy said, "Doing that was as bad as poisoning them. They'll all die, they weren't even weaned. You should have shot them, would've been kinder. Besides, I told you to get your dog neutered months ago." Bubba said, "Just watch the game. Want a beer?"

When Bubba dumped the box of puppies on the ground, the box tipped over and all six puppies tumbled out. For a while, the puppies huddled together and cried. When it began to get dark, all six of them moved towards the trees. In their newness to the woods, they found a place that, though comfortable, wasn't safe. The sky grew dark and a full moon came out. An owl swooped down with its talons outstretched, hooked on to one of the terrified puppies, and flew off with it. The other puppies could hear the sound of the puppy crying, until the sound of the cry blended into the night, and then there were five.

When the long, dark night came to an end, the sun came out and the five puppies became aware of how hungry they were. No matter where they walked, they could not find their mother. They had only recently begun to eat solid foods and, until yesterday, they still relied on Annie for most of their food. The puppies were so hungry that they huddled together and cried. They cried for so long that they became thirsty, as well as hungry. They walked deeper into the woods, looking for their mother and water.

As they walked, they didn't notice that the sun had disappeared behind a layer of clouds. The sky grew dark as night, then suddenly; the five puppies heard the loudest most terrifying sound that they had ever heard. It was so loud that it shook the ground. Along with the noise, a flash of bright light further frightened them. Then the heavens opened up and water fell on them, hard and fast. No matter where they went, the water continued to dump on them. Already afraid, the puppies grew more so by the minute. In their terror, they ran as hard as they could in one direction and then in another, growing more terrified, hungrier, thirstier, and wetter as they ran. After a while, they stopped long enough to drink from a puddle. After so much running, they were so tired that when the rain stopped, they didn't have the energy to find a dry spot to sleep. They settled on a less wet spot and cuddled together to stay warm as they fell in an exhausted sleep, still hungry.

The five puppies woke up to a beautiful warm sunny day the next morning. They were still hungry, but they were no longer wet, cold, or thirsty. The puddle they had found the day before was still where they left it, so they drank from it again. The puppies looked for their mother in earnest, but as they looked, they had another feeling stronger than hunger enter their lives, the feeling of curiosity.

The day was so warm that it didn't take long before there were butterflies flying around them. None of the puppies had ever seen a butterfly before. One of the puppies saw a yellow and orange butterfly and began to chase it, making happy little puppy barks as he ran. The butterfly always flew just ahead of him. He ran harder to try and catch up to it, as the other puppies tried to catch up to him. The butterfly stopped briefly at the end of an old log, at the edge a ravine. The puppy ran onto the old log, but just as he got to the end, the butterfly flew off. The puppy fell off of the log and out into the ravine. He landed on his neck, breaking it. Then, there were four.

The four puppies came to the edge of the ravine and looked down at their brother, not understanding why he wasn't moving. They barked at him, but still he didn't move. After a while, their hunger drew their focus away from their brother to find food. As they hunted, they walked past an old peach tree with peaches covering the ground below it. They had never seen peaches before, but they were so hungry that they tried them. The peaches didn't seem so bad, and there were enough for the puppies to fill their stomachs. Eating the peaches made their stomach's hurt less, but the puppies still missed their mother, so they continued to hunt for her. As night approached, they came to the edge of the trees and found a hole, made by an armadillo. It was dry in the hole, so the four of them squeezed in together and fell fast asleep. While they slept, ticks and fleas covered them. These insects were the kind that carried diseases and killed stronger dogs than these puppies. With almost no food and having fleas and ticks on them, the four puppies grew weaker and were becoming sick.

The puppies got an early start the next morning. As they entered a large field, the puppies saw a large dog in the distance. They ran towards the dog, thinking that it might be their mother. When the puppies got close to the animal, they saw that it wasn't their mother. For some reason they sensed some sort of danger. When they saw the animal move, it moved with a sort of a lope. They turned to run, but it was too late. The animal unknown to them was a coyote, and a hungry one at that. He was on to them in a flash. He jumped the smallest of the puppies, killing her instantly and carrying her off before the other puppies were even aware that the coyote and their sister were gone. Then, there were three.

The three puppies kept looking for their mother through fields and woods, becoming more and more wary of the ever-frightening world that they were thrown in to. The three puppies grew sicker and hungrier. Their bellies had begun to swell and walking became harder. The rain came again, dropping needed water around them, so that they had water to drink. They could not find a dry place to sleep, so the poor sick, hungry, cold and wet puppies huddled together by a big tree as they shivered the night away.

It was hard for the three puppies to get moving the next morning, but after a while it got easier, though they were still shaky. As they slowly walked through a field near some pecan trees, a hawk swooped down from a cloudless sky and snatched another puppy, hardly slowing down. The puppy was so shocked that he hardly had time to give more than a frightened yelp, and in a moment, he was gone. The two remaining puppies were too hungry and sick to notice very much of anything, let alone their brother be taken from them.

Without being aware of it, the two remaining puppies

wandered close to a house near the fields and woods that they had been in since Bubba dumped them out. It was becoming harder for the puppies to walk; they were so tired and hungry. Suddenly, a dog came out from the house and chased the puppies. The puppies found strength to run that they didn't know they had. They ran and screamed like never before. The dog nearly caught them four times. As they ran around the house for the tenth time, they saw a place to hide under a propane tank. Almost as one mind, they both dove under the tank.

It seemed to the puppies that the dog was always out there. Every time they would try to leave the propane tank, he seemed to be close by. The puppies were growing weaker and sicker, so they began to sleep a lot. By the third day, they desperately needed water so they tried to leave the tank. As soon as they took two steps, there was the dog. They were in such bad shape that they began to cry and howl, but quickly ran back under the tank. The dog was surprised by how loud the puppies were and joined them by barking.

With all the noise and commotion that the dog and puppies were making, the puppies almost missed the sound of a human voice. They saw a man and two women crouched down close to them. The puppies, not used to being treated kindly by humans, tried to hide, but they caught them. The puppies were so afraid that they shook. They growled and tried to bite the people, but were so sick that they just didn't have their heart in it.

The man put both puppies in a pen with a place to sleep, water to drink, and some food for them to eat. They had their first real food and sleep in such a long time. For the next two days, both puppies spent most of their time sleeping, eating, and scratching. When they were awake, they hurt. They couldn't eat or drink very much at a time, because when they tried, their stomachs hurt. After a while, drinking water became easier, but their legs and ears hurt and itched.

The man and women took the puppies out of their pen and held each of them closely, talking to them in a soothing and quiet voice. They noticed that neither puppy had much fur, but one had almost none at all whereas the other had enough fur to see that she had two colors of fur. He said, "Let's name these puppies. We should name the puppy I am holding Patch, since its fur has two colors. The other puppy has so little fur, so let's call her Blondie, since what fur we can see seems to be yellow or blonde." Somehow, the puppies felt more secure.

The man and women brought the puppies to tubs of warm water, and the women gently placed each puppy into the tubs and, using warm rags, gave them their first baths. The man pulled off over thirty ticks from each dog. After their baths and the tick removal, the puppies felt better and for the first time in their lives, they felt loved. They were still sick, still couldn't eat much, and could no longer walk very much either, but they felt better.

For the next two days the two puppies looked like they were feeling better. For the first time since she was with her mother, Patch began to wag her tail when the man or the women came near her. On the third day, things took a turn for the worst. Blondie stopped eating and by the fifth day, Blondie took her last breath. Then, there was one.

Patch was moved in to the house, but Patch grieved for her sister for two days. She stood by the door refusing to eat, never waging her tail, and always staring outside. After three months, Patch recovered completely, though she remained timid her whole life. She was to become a beloved family member of the family who rescued her and a good friend of the dog who chased her.

Some heroes wear blue jeans, some wear suits, but still others wear the coats that they were born with. Heroes in our midst are not limited to the human kind, but can be found in the animal kingdom as well. There are so many stories of animals being heroes and many just about dogs doing heroic actions. What motivates the dogs in these stories? Love does, love is the greatest motivation for any hero. We are in the midst of heroes, all we have to do is to look for them.

# SCHOOL

# STUPIDEST STUDENT EVER

CHARLEY WAS IN Junior High School. He had learning disabilities, but he was unaware of them; he only knew that he didn't do well in school. His brothers and sisters were all very good at school and everyone expected him to be just as good, but quickly, it was evident that he wasn't. His counselor told him he had great potential, but he wasn't using his brain enough. He wasn't trying hard enough and needed to put out more effort.

What Charley didn't know, was when he read words, the letters in the words would change. He could limp along with reading, because there were always enough words that he could read that helped him understand what he was reading. It was worth the struggle for him to read, because reading was an escape for Charley, an escape from the sadness of his learning disabilities. Math was another story. He had no way of knowing it, but when he looked at numbers on paper in math, the numbers would change. When he was tired, his learning disabilities grew worse. Charley was tired of being thought of as stupid, so he studied hard for a math test. He studied late into the night the night before his exam, not knowing the more tired he became, the more his numbers would change. Before he fell asleep, he knew the formulas back and forth, he knew how to check his answers, and he never felt more ready for an exam. Unfortunately, he studied far too long and only got four hours of sleep.

His exam was first period, and although he was tired, he had more confidence than he ever remembered having before the test began. As soon as he had completed the first problem and checked the answer, he found it was wrong. He tried it again, and had another answer and it too was wrong. Something was terribly wrong, but he didn't know what was making it so wrong. He tried again and still, there was another answer and it was wrong as well. His numbers were changing, but he had no way of knowing it. As the clock ticked away and the time was getting short, he panicked and made it worse. When the test was down to the last minute, he no longer trusted what he had learned from studying. He heard the teacher say, "Time is up. Everyone turn in your test." Charley couldn't give his teacher his test; he was too ashamed and too beaten to turn it in.

Half way through the day, Charley heard from his friends in the second and third periods how his teacher was telling the class that Charley was the stupidest student she had ever taught. In period five, it took all of his courage to talk to her in front of thirty other students and tell her that telling her other student that he was stupid was wrong. She told him that he was stupid, too stupid to turn in his test, where she would have given him ten points for his name and ten points for the date. In spite of himself, he cried. His teacher, along with most of the thirty students in the class, laughed at him.

Charley wasn't stupid. He was, in fact, very intelligent, but his learning disabilities got in his way. But for a while, Charley believed what his teacher and others that echoed his teacher said about him. Even his family believed that he was lazy and not trying. They weren't even sure if he would graduate from high school, much less college. It took Charley three years to fight back, but he didn't fight it alone. Another teacher believed in him and taught him how to adapt to his reading challenges. It took another ten years to adapt to his math challenges. Among the many lessons he learned on how bridge his learning disabilities, there were four that were crucial to his academic success; 1) He had to be well rested before he took any test. 2) He learned how to take tests. 3) To do well in taking tests and to write, he had to sit with both feet flat on the floor and with his back straight. 4) He had to work every math problem, until he came up with the same answer four times.

Charley failed the math class with the teacher who called him stupid, but he passed the summer school class he took, which allowed him to be promoted to the next grade. He went out of his way to avoid seeing his teacher as long as he was in the school where she taught, then saw her only a couple of times when he went to the nearby high school. After he graduated from high school, he moved thousands of miles away from the teacher who called him the stupidest student she had ever taught, and never saw her again. Some years later, he even studied to be a teacher, vowing that he would never be the kind of a teacher his math teacher was that he would be a better teacher than she ever was. He became much more of a teacher than she ever could be, and because of his kind heart, he went on to teach special education.

His teacher had no idea of how much damage she did to Charley, or how much she had inspired him. Every one of us has choices to make. We can choose to accept the challenges we face, or let those challenges destroy us; the choice is ours.

Heroes aren't always heroes because they rescue someone else; sometimes they are heroes because they rescue themselves. By saving themselves, they open the door to helping others later. There are thousands, even hundreds of thousands, of people just like Charley, none of them wearing capes; some of them are just wearing blue jeans. Where are the heroes in our midst? We are in the midst of heroes; we just need to look for them.

# HEROES ON THE ROAD

HENRIETTA IS RESPONSIBLE for seventy-one treasures while guiding twelve tons of metal, a mobile bullet if you will, of about thirty-seven feet long by eight feet wide. It is capable of reaching speeds of up to fifty-five miles per hour that has the potential to ruin at least seven hundred lives. To guide this huge bullet, she has to always be alert, scanning from side to side as far as she can see, forward, and even behind her, using mirrors to aid in seeing where she cannot see by turning her head. In addition, her hearing has to be at its peak, because she has to listen for sounds of problems inside the bullet she is in charge of for potential problems that might cause it to go out of control. She faces countless crises that must be resolved, even as her focus is on many different challenges. The volume inside is way beyond loud, yet she needs to always be listening for sounds that could be dangerous enough for the bullet to go out of control, or the treasures inside of it to be harmed in any way . Her memory has to be very sharp because she has to make the extremely heavy and potentially dangerous vehicle come to a complete stop. Henrietta is a school bus driver.

Every school day, mothers and fathers trust the men and women who drive school buses to transport the most precious part of their lives to and from school. They expect and demand that they will do so safely. They have reason to expect the school bus drivers will treat their responsibility with respect. These men and women have the same behavior management challenges that teachers in classrooms face, except with the added danger of being in a moving environment. They know that in an instant, the precious lives that have been entrusted to them could be at risk. Inside the bus, safety issues can occur suddenly.

Among the many that can and do include; disagreements that flare up that lead to fights while the bus is moving, children getting sick, and some children who release their energy by moving around the bus. With all that bus drivers are responsible for, they rarely hear a thank you from the precious lives they care for, or from the ones who entrust their children to them. Though away from their buses, teachers will often hear students talk about their favorite bus drivers, but not close enough for their bus drivers to hear the praises themselves.

School bus drivers' jobs are among the most difficult and challenging in education. Those who drive our school buses could be called guides and mobile life guards for the treasures that parents entrust them with. When called upon, they are trained to perform CPR or save lives of students suffering from allergic reactions. They are not highly paid and rarely get recognition for what they do, yet they are heroes in our midst. Most don't wear uniforms, but some do; some even wear blue jeans.

*During the 2008 school year in the United States, there were six hundred forty-seven thousand five hundred school bus drivers who delivered about forty-five million nine hundred seventy-two thousand five hundred students to and from school every day. These heroes are safely driving school buses on our roads before sun up, much of the school year, and late afternoon. They drive high into the mountains and deep into valleys. They are found on heavily traveled highways and rarely traveled country roads. They are at every high school athletic event and even at special community events. Where are the heroes? Almost forty-six million are driving yellow school buses on our roads twice a day every school day. We are in the midst of heroes; all we have to do is to look for them, even when we are driving.*

# AUTHOR BIO

K EVIN EWING WAS born in North Tonawanda, New York
Mr. Ewing lived in California & Washington State. He currently resides in Georgia.

Besides being an author Mr. Ewing has enjoyed many careers such as production controller, salesman, financial planner, pest & weed controller, funeral insurance salesman, footwear manager, and driving instructor. For the last fifteen years he has been a special education teacher primarily working with students who have profound mental challenges.

His Education is as follows: North Tonawanda High School Regents diploma, Santa Barbara City College-AA degree in general studies, Washington State University-BA Education. Central Washington University M Ed.

His college Associations: Omicron Delta Kappa, Phi Delta Kappa

Mr. Ewing is certainly a true family man. He has been married for 30 years to his lovely wife Reva. He has four beautiful children. Ronald age 24, Mara age 22, Juliann age 20 & Collin age 17.

Please see our growing catalog, at:

# www.WheelManPress.com

www.ingramcontent.com/pod-product-compliance
Lightning Source LLC
Chambersburg PA
CBHW052135170626
46812CB00004B/1429